GIADA
AT HOME

GIADA
AT HOME

FAMILY RECIPES FROM
ITALY AND CALIFORNIA

GIADA DE LAURENTIIS

PHOTOGRAPHS BY JONELLE WEAVER

Clarkson Potter/Publishers
New York

Library of Congress Cataloging-in-Publication Data
De Laurentiis, Giada.
Giada at home / Giada De Laurentiis. — 1st ed.
1. Cookery, Italian. I. Title.
TX723.D3267 2010
641.5945—dc22   2009029147
ISBN 978-0-307-45101-9

Printed in the United States of America

Design by Marysarah Quinn

10 9 8 7 6 5 4 3 2 1

First Edition

To my beautiful daughter, Jade,
who fills each day with such
joy and makes this journey
for Todd and me so
much more fun

contents

introduction

It's often been said that to find the best food in Italy you need to be invited to someone's house for a home-cooked meal. It's those simple dishes, lovingly prepared and designed to make good use of what is seasonal, available, and affordable—even leftovers—that have always been my favorites and have most strongly influenced the way I cook at home to this day. I think of those dishes as "old world" cooking, and they remain staples of my repertoire.

They're also the dishes I grew up eating, both as a child living in Italy and then throughout my teen years in this country. Over time, though, the dishes themselves evolved. As a child I rarely ate avocados, pineapple, or jalapeño peppers; and beef, easily the most popular red meat in this country, had been a more occasional food for us in Italy, taking a backseat to lamb and veal. And while we'd eaten plenty of pork in the form of sausage and cured meat, rarely did we sit down to a big plate of the pan-fried pork chops or roasts that seemed to be a mealtime staple at all my friends' homes. At the same time, some of the foods we'd taken for granted in Italy, like lentils, fennel, and mascarpone cheese, almost never appeared in American kitchens, and really it's only in the last decade or so that these ingredients and others, such as broccoli rabe or farro, have become widely available. So, ever resourceful and creative, my mother adapted our family favorites to incorporate what she found at the market while retaining the spirit of the original Italian recipes. Her way of combining the best of the old world and the new has been the inspiration for many of the recipes I create now to serve my own family.

The shape of the meal itself also changed over the years in our household, evolving from a multicourse extravaganza that might take a couple of hours even on a weeknight to a streamlined meal more in keeping with the faster pace of life here. At first it seemed strange to have meat, vegetables, even pasta, served all at once and all on the same plate, or to see foods I thought of primarily as snacks, like soups or sandwiches, taking center stage. But I also came to appreciate the

fact that meals could be lighter and less filling; a salad based on grains or beautiful vegetables and a bit of cooked meat or seafood was completely satisfying and didn't fill me up and slow me down the way a plate of pasta followed by a meat course might.

Of course we still follow the tradition of weekly meals with my extended family to this day, and on those occasions we rarely veer from the long-established blueprint of antipasti followed by pasta, then a meat or fish course, and a final taste of something sweet. Throughout my childhood pasta or grains were served at both lunch *and* dinner, just as they are to this day throughout most of Italy, and even now no meal in my grandfather's home would be considered complete without it. I cherish those meals as much for the togetherness and wonderful conversations we share as for the food; but I also recognize that kind of closeness is nurtured by the leisurely pace and comfortable mood created by the slow, delicious progression of the food itself, and I'd never want to change that.

Now that Todd and I have started our own family, we observe both traditions at home. Some nights (or mornings in the case of brunch) allow for a bit more time, and a more relaxed approach to cooking and eating. That's when I think back to the recipes I still remember fondly from my childhood, or have since discovered on my travels throughout Italy. I try not to alter these recipes too much, preferring to prepare the dishes much as Italian mothers have been doing for hundreds of years, and sharing a little bit of my family history with Jade now that she's old enough to eat along with me and Todd.

Other times, I get inspired by a trip to the farmer's market or by a beautiful piece of fish at the seafood counter, and I want to focus on dishes that allow those clean, fresh flavors to shine. Sometimes, after a long day, a flavorful pasta or a substantial salad is all any of us needs or wants. For those nights I've built up a repertoire of quick and easy dishes that reflect my adoptive home in California, the food traditions that my husband and our friends have brought to our table, *and* my Italian heritage.

Now I've found myself simplifying the kitchen experience even more without compromising the taste, look, and overall feel of the food. But I don't think that's a bad thing. Much as I appreciate the skill and artistry of a chef working at the top of his or her game when I go out for a meal, in a home setting it can seem over the top. Which is not to say that I don't occasionally pull out the stops when we entertain or if I'm making a special family meal. But I'm always mindful of the fact that turning a home-cooked meal into something straight out of a restaurant negates the warmth of the setting and the fact that I've decided to open my home and share my family. As long as the food tastes amazing and I've devoted a bit of attention to how it looks on the plate, I know even my most discerning friends will appreciate the effort I've made—as well as the fact that I'm not too tired to sit down and enjoy it with them!

And certainly there have never been more good reasons to cook at home. For some of us the expense of eating out has moved from the frequent to the occasional category in the monthly budget; cooking at home is a far less costly way to spend time with friends than eating at a fancy restaurant. Others of us are concerned about the quality of the ingredients we feed our family, and cooking at home, with food you've chosen with care from trusted sources—maybe even from the farmer who raised it—ensures you know exactly what you are eating.

But all those good reasons aside, home cooking is a way to express your love for family and friends, and to make time in your life, no matter how full, for togetherness and new traditions. I hope this book will encourage you to spend a bit more time around the table, and to enjoy every moment—and every bite.

NOTE: Classic recipe titles are set in orange and have this symbol: ❁.
Modern recipe titles are set in green.

appetizers

Cheese-Stuffed Dates with Prosciutto ✿

Italian Fried Olives ✿

Whole-Wheat Pita Chips with Mascarpone-Chive Dip

Roasted Eggplant and White Bean Crostini ✿

Artichoke and Bean Bruschetta ✿

Pea Pesto Crostini

Tomato Basil Tartlets

Stuffed Baby Peppers ✿

Smoked Salmon and Apple Carpaccio

Sautéed Shrimp Cocktail

Fried Cheese-Stuffed Zucchini Blossoms ✿

Beef Skewers with Cherry Tomatoes and Parsley Sauce

In this country appetizers are synonymous with restaurant food or party fare; but Italians take a much more relaxed approach to starters. Even a casual meal at home generally begins with an antipasto or two, something colorful and light that can be eaten in a couple of bites, perhaps on a small toast slice. While some antipasti may include fish or perhaps a bit of cured meat, most are vegetable based and reflect the seasons. Either way they are a beautiful and delicious way to start off a meal without filling you up.

I love to set out my own spread of antipasti for a cocktail gathering or a casual dinner, and classic bar snacks like Italian Fried Olives (page 18), which are easy to pop in your mouth, and Fried Cheese-Stuffed Zucchini Blossoms (page 37) are a big hit. I always include at least one kind of crostini or bruschetta, and I top them with something brightly flavored and fresh tasting, like green pea pesto; the vibrant green color is so appealing. For a more formal affair, though, I like to do a plated first course, giving one of my favorite Italian dishes an update. Carpaccio, for instance, is typically made with meat, but I prefer to use smoked salmon; it's light and clean, and it's readily available all year long.

cheese-stuffed dates
with prosciutto
4 TO 6 SERVINGS

The sweetest, best kind of dates are Medjools. They're large, so they are easy to fill, meaty, and chewy. Stuffed with goat cheese and wrapped in prosciutto, they provide a perfect sweet-salty mouthful in every bite. Serve these with a crisp white wine as the ideal before-dinner tidbit.

- 1/4 cup (2 ounces) goat cheese, at room temperature
- 1/4 cup (2 ounces) mascarpone cheese, at room temperature
- 1/4 cup finely chopped fresh basil leaves
- Salt and freshly ground black pepper
- 16 Medjool dates (12 ounces)
- 8 thin slices prosciutto, halved lengthwise

special equipment

- 16 toothpicks or cocktail picks

In a small bowl, mix together the cheeses and basil. Season with salt and pepper.

With a knife, make a lengthwise incision in each date. Gently open the dates slightly and remove the pits. Spoon about ½ teaspoon cheese mixture inside each one. Close the dates around the filling. Wrap a piece of prosciutto around each date and secure with a toothpick.

Arrange the stuffed dates on a platter and serve.

italian fried olives

Olives stuffed with cheese and fried are a classic bar snack commonly found in Naples and in Sicily. I like to mix the Gorgonzola with a bit of ricotta to tame its strong flavor. Unlike most fried foods, these can be made ahead of time and they will still be delicious a good while later. Pile them on a platter for a party and watch them disappear.

1/4	cup (1 ounce) crumbled Gorgonzola cheese, at room temperature
1/4	cup whole-milk ricotta cheese, at room temperature
1 1/2	teaspoons dried thyme
1 1/2	teaspoons grated lemon zest (from 1 lemon)
20	pitted medium to large green olives, rinsed and thoroughly dried
1/4	cup all-purpose flour
1	large egg
1/2	cup plain dried bread crumbs
	Vegetable oil, for frying

special equipment

A pastry bag fitted with a 1/4-inch round plain tip

In a small bowl, combine the cheeses, thyme, and lemon zest. Spoon into the pastry bag. Pipe the cheese mixture into each olive.

Put the flour into a small bowl. Lightly beat the egg in another small bowl and put the bread crumbs in a third small bowl. Working in batches, dredge the olives in the flour. Using a slotted spoon, remove the olives and place in the bowl with the beaten egg. Coat the olives with the egg and then transfer to the bowl of bread crumbs. Coat the olives with the bread crumbs.

In a large heavy-bottomed saucepan, pour enough oil to fill the pan about a third of the way. Heat over medium heat until a deep-frying thermometer inserted in the oil reaches 350°F. (If you don't have a thermometer, toss in a cube of bread; it will brown in about 3 minutes and, when it does, the oil is ready.) Fry the olives, in batches, for 30 to 45 seconds, until golden brown. Drain the fried olives on paper towels. Cool for at least 5 minutes before serving.

whole-wheat pita chips
with mascarpone-chive dip

4 TO 6 SERVINGS

It's no secret that I love mascarpone cheese—and who doesn't love bacon? Stir them together and you have a super-creamy, elegant dip that tastes like the most decadently topped baked potato you've ever had. The mix is surprisingly versatile, too: thin it down a bit with milk and use it as a dressing for greens or a sauce for salmon or chicken.

4	whole-wheat pita breads
2	tablespoons olive oil
1	teaspoon dried oregano
	Salt and freshly ground black pepper
4	strips bacon, cooked until crisp, finely chopped
1	cup (8 ounces) mascarpone cheese, at room temperature
3/4	cup sour cream
1/4	cup chopped fresh chives

Place an oven rack in the center of the oven and preheat the oven to 450°F.

Cut each pita into 8 wedges. Arrange the pita wedges in a single layer on a rimmed baking sheet. Brush with the oil, then sprinkle with the oregano, ½ teaspoon salt, and ½ teaspoon pepper. Bake for 5 to 8 minutes, until crisp and golden. Set aside to cool.

In a medium bowl, combine the bacon, mascarpone cheese, sour cream, and chives. Season with salt and pepper. Transfer the dip to a serving bowl.

Arrange the pita chips and dip on a platter and serve.

bruschetta
& crostini

The terms *bruschetta* and *crostini* are often used interchangeably. But while both refer to a piece of grilled or toasted bread with a savory topping and are typically served as antipasti, there are in fact differences between the two, namely in size and presentation.

The word *bruschetta* comes from the Italian verb *bruscare*, which means to roast over hot coals. Grilling thick slices of bread and then rubbing them with garlic or half of a tomato was a common way for frugal housewives to extend the life of stale bread. Over time bruschetta evolved into more than just grilled bread, as ingredients such as prosciutto, mozzarella, roasted peppers, and cured meats were added to the toppings. Because the base is a fairly large, thick bread slice, bruschetta tends to have a more rustic appearance and can stand up to hearty toppings; it may be eaten by hand but can also be served on a plate with a knife and fork.

Crostini, on the other hand, are more often toasted in the oven than grilled, and tend to be smaller and thinner. These "little toasts" make perfect one-bite hors d'oeuvres, but topped with cheese and melted under the broiler they're also great to float on a bowl of soup, crouton-style, or serve with a salad. Because they are smaller and more refined, they are perfect for richer, more sophisticated toppings than you might serve on heartier bruschetta.

For bruschetta, I prefer to use ciabatta bread or a pane rustica because the loaves are wide but flat and not too dense. Slicing the bread crosswise into ½- or ¾-inch-thick slices makes long narrow toasts that won't droop or sag under their topping when picked up. I generally use a baguette for my crostini and cut them fairly straight across to make small, nicely rounded toasts of uniform size that look beautiful arranged on a tray or platter.

roasted eggplant and white bean crostini

4 TO 6 SERVINGS

This is rustic and simple, and deeply satisfying. Pureed beans can get a bit crusty when exposed to air, so if you make these ahead of time, drizzle a bit of a nice fruity olive oil over each crostini to keep it fresh and make it glisten. If you want a lighter version, you can certainly serve this on cucumber rounds, but I love the way the smoky flavor of the eggplant and the grilled bread work together.

1   (1½-pound) eggplant or 3 Japanese eggplants, trimmed and cut into 2-inch pieces

⅓   cup olive oil, plus more for drizzling
     Salt and freshly ground black pepper

1   French baguette, cut into ½-inch-thick slices

1   (15-ounce) can cannellini beans, drained and rinsed

⅓   cup loosely packed fresh flat-leaf parsley leaves

3   tablespoons fresh lemon juice (from 1 lemon)

1   garlic clove

Place an oven rack in the middle of the oven and preheat the oven to 450°F.

Put the eggplant on a parchment paper–lined rimmed baking sheet. Drizzle with olive oil and season with salt and pepper. Roast for 20 to 25 minutes, until golden brown. Set aside to cool.

While the eggplant is roasting, preheat a grill pan over medium-high heat. Drizzle the bread slices with olive oil on both sides and arrange in the pan. Cook until both sides are pale golden and crisp, about 5 minutes total. Set aside to cool.

In the bowl of a food processor, combine the cooled eggplant (flesh and skin), beans, parsley, lemon juice, garlic, ½ teaspoon salt, and ¼ teaspoon pepper. Pulse until the mixture is coarsely chopped. With the machine running, gradually add the ⅓ cup olive oil and process until the mixture is creamy. Season with salt and pepper, if needed.

Spoon the spread into a small bowl and serve with the bread slices. Alternatively, spoon the spread over the bread and arrange on a serving platter.

artichoke and bean bruschetta

4 TO 6 SERVINGS

Rome is famous for its artichokes, and in the Jewish district you can buy amazing fried whole artichokes on street corners. Back home, I use frozen artichokes for ease and I love combining them with beans in a creamy dip for bruschetta, a favorite snack throughout Italy. The crispy, salty prosciutto highlights the subtle flavor of the artichokes and adds crunch.

	Vegetable oil cooking spray
4	very thin slices prosciutto
12	(¼-inch-thick) slices rustic country bread
½	cup olive oil, plus more for drizzling
1	(12-ounce) package frozen artichoke hearts, thawed
1	(15-ounce) can cannellini beans, rinsed and drained
1	cup freshly grated Pecorino Romano cheese
½	cup coarsely chopped fresh basil leaves
1	teaspoon grated lemon zest
1	tablespoon fresh lemon juice
2	teaspoons salt
½	teaspoon freshly ground black pepper

Place an oven rack in the center of the oven and preheat the oven to 375°F. Spray a rimmed baking sheet with vegetable oil cooking spray.

Lay the prosciutto in a single layer on the prepared baking sheet and bake for 10 to 12 minutes, until crispy. Set aside to cool for 10 minutes.

On another baking sheet, arrange the bread slices in a single layer. Using a pastry brush, brush the bread with ¼ cup of the oil. Bake for 12 to 15 minutes, until golden.

In a food processor, combine the artichoke hearts, beans, cheese, basil, lemon zest, lemon juice, salt, and pepper. Pulse until the mixture is chunky. With the machine running, slowly add the remaining ¼ cup olive oil and mix until combined but still slightly chunky.

Spoon the artichoke mixture onto the crostini. Crumble the prosciutto and sprinkle on top. Drizzle with oil and serve.

pea pesto crostini

4 TO 6 SERVINGS

I don't keep a lot in my freezer, but one thing you'll always find there is a package of frozen peas. They're sweet, they have a lovely green color, and when puréed they can satisfy a craving for a starchy food. If you're not a big fan of peas, at least give this a try. I think it's going to be your new favorite thing. I can't resist eating it straight out of the bowl!

1	(10-ounce) package frozen peas, thawed
1	garlic clove
1/2	cup freshly grated Parmesan cheese
1	teaspoon salt, plus more to taste
1/4	teaspoon freshly ground black pepper, plus more to taste
2/3	cup olive oil
8	(1/2-inch-thick) slices whole-grain baguette or ciabatta bread, preferably day-old (see Cook's Note)
8	cherry tomatoes, halved, or 1 small tomato, diced

For the pea pesto: Pulse together in a food processor the peas, garlic, Parmesan cheese, salt, and pepper. With the machine running, slowly add 1/3 cup of the olive oil and continue to mix until well combined, 1 to 2 minutes. Season with more salt and pepper, if needed. Transfer to a small bowl and set aside.

For the crostini: Preheat a stovetop griddle or grill pan over medium-high.

Brush both sides of each of the bread slices with the remaining 1/3 cup olive oil and grill until golden, 1 to 2 minutes. Transfer the bread to a platter and spread 1 to 2 tablespoons pesto on each slice. Top each crostini with 2 tomato halves and serve.

COOK'S NOTE: Day-old bread works best here because it stands up to the pea purée and isn't too soft in the center. If you don't have any on hand, you can dry out fresh bread by putting the slices in a 300°F oven until slightly crisp, about 5 minutes.

tomato basil tartlets

When it comes to cocktail food, I like one-biters and I like things that are dainty and beautiful. These pretty little tarts fit that bill and more. They taste as fantastic as they look. I prefer to use black-olive tapenade because of its richness, but you can certainly try green-olive, which is tangier.

1   (10 x 9-inch) sheet frozen puff pastry, thawed
    All-purpose flour, for sprinkling
1/3 cup store-bought black-olive tapenade
1   cup (2 ounces) grated Fontina cheese
8   cherry tomatoes, quartered
6   fresh basil leaves, chopped
    Fleur de sel or other coarse sea salt (optional)

special equipment

A 2¼-inch-round cookie cutter

Place an oven rack in the center of the oven and preheat the oven to 400°F. Line a baking sheet with parchment paper.

Unroll the puff pastry on a lightly floured work surface. Using the tines of a fork, prick the pastry all over. Using a 2¼-inch-round cookie cutter, cut out 16 rounds of pastry. Place the pastry rounds ¾ inch apart on the prepared baking sheet. Lay a piece of parchment paper on top of the pastry rounds and then place another baking sheet directly on top of the parchment paper to keep the pastry even while baking. Bake for 10 to 12 minutes, until golden. Remove the top baking sheet and the top piece of parchment paper.

Spread 1 teaspoon tapenade on each pastry round. Spoon about 1 tablespoon cheese on top. Arrange 2 tomato quarters over each dollop of cheese. Bake for 5 to 7 minutes, until the cheese has melted.

Transfer the tartlets to a platter and sprinkle them with chopped basil and some fleur de sel, if desired.

stuffed baby peppers

4 TO 6 SERVINGS

My mother always loved to serve stuffed vegetables; she stuffed zucchini, potatoes, onions, and, of course, all kinds of peppers. It may have been her way of getting us to eat our vegetables, but we loved them so much we ate them right out of the fridge the next day. I've used pancetta in the filling, but this is an easy recipe to vary and you could certainly substitute ground beef, sausage—almost anything savory that you like. These taste better the longer they sit, so they make great leftovers.

	Vegetable oil cooking spray
2	tablespoons olive oil
3	ounces thinly sliced pancetta, finely chopped
½	medium onion, finely chopped
¾	cup whole-milk ricotta cheese
⅓	cup freshly grated Parmesan cheese
½	cup frozen petite peas, thawed
	Salt and freshly ground black pepper
24	(2- to 3-inch long) sweet baby peppers

Place an oven rack in the center of the oven and preheat the oven to 350°F. Spray a rimmed baking sheet with vegetable oil cooking spray. Set aside.

In a medium skillet, heat the olive oil over medium-high heat. Add the pancetta and cook, stirring frequently, until brown and crispy, 5 to 7 minutes. Using a slotted spoon, remove the pancetta and drain on paper towels. Add the onion to the pan and cook until translucent and soft, about 5 minutes. Set aside to cool for 10 minutes.

In a medium bowl, combine the onion, pancetta, cheeses, and peas. Season with salt and pepper.

Using a paring knife, cut ½ inch from the stem end of each pepper. Remove the seeds and veins. Using a small dessert spoon, fill each pepper with the cheese mixture. Place the filled peppers on the prepared baking sheet and bake for 15 to 18 minutes, until the peppers begin to soften and the cheese is warmed through. Cool for 10 minutes.

Arrange the peppers on a platter and serve.

COOK'S NOTE: To serve as an entrée portion, double the filling, stuff it into 4 full-size bell peppers, and bake at 350ºF for 1 hour, covering with foil if they brown too much, until the peppers are just starting to collapse.

smoked salmon and apple carpaccio
4 TO 6 SERVINGS

When I go to a restaurant and want something light, I immediately look to the carpaccios and crudos, which often feature marinated raw fish. Smoked salmon can deliver the same light, clean flavors but without the worry of serving raw beef or fish at home. I like to arrange the salmon and apples on a platter and let guests pile them onto slices of bread themselves; the color of the salmon is simply stunning next to the green apples, which also contribute crunch and freshness.

6	(¼-inch-thick) slices rosemary or olive bread, quartered
	Juice of 1 lemon
1	small green apple, such as Granny Smith, halved, cored, and very thinly sliced
6	ounces Nova Scotia smoked salmon
1	tablespoon capers, rinsed and drained
	Olive oil, for drizzling
	Salt and freshly ground black pepper

Place an oven rack in the center of the oven and preheat the oven to 400°F.

Arrange the bread on a baking sheet in a single layer. Bake for 10 to 12 minutes, until lightly brown and crisp. Cool to room temperature, about 10 minutes.

To prevent the apples from browning, in a small bowl, combine 2 cups water with the lemon juice. Add the apple slices and soak until ready to use. Drain and blot with paper towels just before using.

Arrange the smoked salmon in a single layer on a serving platter. Lay the apple slices on top. Sprinkle the capers over the salmon and apple slices. Drizzle with olive oil and season with salt and pepper. Serve with the toasted bread.

sautéed shrimp cocktail

4 TO 6 SERVINGS

The sight of a platter of jumbo shrimp at a party always makes guests happy, but the usual shrimp cocktail is served ice-cold and, in my opinion, is pretty flavorless. I think shrimp taste so much better served warm—especially with this simple and colorful dipping sauce to dunk them into. The ingredients are an interesting combination, and their unique flavors, along with the color of the turmeric, yield a creamy, tangy, and slightly sweet sauce.

2	tablespoons olive oil
1	pound jumbo shrimp, peeled but tail left on, deveined
1	tablespoon herbes de Provence
	Salt and freshly ground black pepper
1¼	cups plain yogurt
2	tablespoons mayonnaise
2	tablespoons whole-grain mustard
1½	tablespoons pure maple syrup
1	teaspoon turmeric
¼	cup chopped fresh basil leaves

In a large skillet, heat the oil over medium-high heat. Add the shrimp and herbes de Provence. Season with salt and pepper. Cook until the shrimp are pink and cooked through, about 2 minutes on each side. Remove from the heat.

In a small bowl, mix together the yogurt, mayonnaise, mustard, maple syrup, turmeric, and basil. Season with salt and pepper.

Arrange the shrimp on a serving platter with the bowl of dip in the center.

fried cheese-stuffed zucchini blossoms

MAKES 8 BLOSSOMS; 4 SERVINGS

Delicate and beautiful zucchini blossoms make their appearance at farmer's markets in mid- to late summer. In Italy, the blossoms are stuffed with just about anything and prepared in a number of ways, from sautéed to baked, or just served fresh in a salad. My favorite is and always has been stuffed and fried—and served with a side of marinara sauce.

1	cup all-purpose flour
1	cup sparkling water
	Salt
1/3	cup (3 ounces) goat cheese, at room temperature
2	tablespoons (1 ounce) cream cheese, at room temperature
2	teaspoons heavy cream
1	tablespoon chopped fresh basil leaves
1	scallion, white part only, finely chopped
	Freshly ground black pepper
8	zucchini blossoms (see Cook's Note), stamens removed
	Vegetable oil, for frying

In a medium bowl, whisk together the flour, water, and ¾ teaspoon salt until smooth. Set the batter aside.

In a small bowl combine the goat cheese, cream cheese, heavy cream, basil, and scallion. Mix until smooth. Season with salt and pepper. Spoon 1½ to 2 teaspoons filling into each blossom. Close the blossoms and gently twist the petals to seal.

In a large heavy-bottomed saucepan, pour enough oil to fill the pan about a third of the way. Heat over medium heat until a deep-frying thermometer inserted in the oil reaches 350°F. (If you don't have a thermometer, toss in a cube of bread; it will brown in about 3 minutes and, when it does, the oil is ready.) Dip the stuffed zucchini blossoms in the batter and allow any excess to drip off. Fry for 1 to 2 minutes, turning occasionally, until golden brown. Drain the cooked blossoms on paper towels.

Season with salt and serve warm.

beef skewers with cherry tomatoes and parsley sauce

4 TO 6 SERVINGS

Beef filet always makes an occasion special, but in the case of these mini beef kebabs it's the parsley sauce—almost a fresh salsa—that makes the dish shine. For an interesting change, mix it up and substitute fresh pineapple chunks for the tomatoes; they make for a surprisingly harmonious combination. One note: Don't marinate the beef any longer than three hours because the vinegar in the marinade will break down the meat and ruin its texture.

3	cups fresh flat-leaf parsley leaves
2	garlic cloves
2	tablespoons red wine vinegar
1	teaspoon crushed red pepper flakes
1	teaspoon sugar
	Salt and freshly ground black pepper
1/2	cup olive oil
1 1/2	pounds beef filet, cut into 3/4-inch cubes (about 40 cubes)
	Vegetable or canola oil, for the grill
40	cherry tomatoes (about 2 pints)

special equipment

20	(8-inch) wooden or bamboo skewers, soaked in water for 30 minutes

In the bowl of a food processor, blend together the parsley, garlic, vinegar, red pepper flakes, sugar, 1½ teaspoons salt, and ½ teaspoon black pepper, until smooth. With the machine running, gradually add the olive oil and process until incorporated. Spoon half of the sauce into a medium bowl. Spoon the remaining sauce in a small serving bowl; cover with plastic wrap and refrigerate until ready to serve.

Put the beef in the medium bowl with the parsley sauce. Toss well to coat the beef. Cover and refrigerate for at least 30 minutes and up to 3 hours.

Place a grill pan over medium-high heat or preheat a gas or charcoal grill. Lightly oil the grill pan or the grilling rack with vegetable oil.

Thread the skewers starting with a cherry tomato, then a cube of beef. Repeat with another cherry tomato and another cube of beef. Continue with the remaining skewers. Grill the skewers for 2 to 3 minutes on each side (for medium-rare) or until desired doneness. Season with salt and pepper.

To serve, arrange the beef skewers on a serving platter. Drizzle with the reserved parsley sauce or serve the sauce on the side as a condiment.

soups & sandwiches

Chicken, Artichoke, and Cannellini Bean Spezzatino ❁

Ligurian Fish Stew ❁

White Bean and Chicken Chili

Butternut Squash Soup with Fontina Cheese Crostini ❁

Lemon Chicken Soup with Spaghetti

Grilled Vegetable, Herb, and Goat Cheese Sandwiches

Piadina with Fontina and Prosciutto ❁

Zucchini and Olive Pizza ❁

Chicken Burgers with Garlic-Rosemary Mayonnaise

Mini Italian Pub Burgers

Open-Faced Tuna Sandwiches with Arugula
    and Sweet-Pickle Mayonnaise

Caponata Panini ❁

Given the common presence of panini on American menus these days you might be surprised to learn that Italians are not really big sandwich eaters. In Italy sandwiches are regarded as snack food, something to munch on between meals, rather than a meal in their own right. Soup, too, is considered the kind of thing you'd eat to stave off hunger pangs between real meals, or if you were under the weather—quite a difference from this country, where hamburgers rule the roost and a steaming bowl of soup is many people's idea of the perfect cold-weather meal.

Despite their secondary status, though, soups and sandwiches exist in every region of Italy, and whether they're served as a snack, Italian-style, or as the main event, I find they make an ideal lunch or light supper, just as is. Spezzatino, a hearty stew brimming with chicken, cannellini beans, and artichokes, is a substantial dish that needs only a salad to complete it, and Piadina with Fontina and Prosciutto (page 60) has all the ingredients and characteristics to satisfy a meal. Soups and sandwiches also provide the perfect playground for old world–new world crossovers, like my Caponata Panini (page 68), savory pressed sandwiches filled with an eggplant mixture more commonly served as a condiment for meats in Italy, or my chicken soup, which is even more sustaining and delicious with the addition of broken pieces of spaghetti, a trick my mother used to bulk up soups such as minestrone and use up odds and ends. And of course I couldn't resist giving the all-American burger an Italian-style makeover, substituting chicken for beef and adding fresh herbs like rosemary and parsley. After all, Italians might not eat a lot of burgers, but we make a lot of meatballs!

chicken, artichoke, and cannellini bean spezzatino

4 TO 6 SERVINGS

Spezzatino is an Italian vegetable stew that has meat in it. This one boasts small bites of chicken and a sprinkle of crunchy pancetta. I love artichokes, so I add them, along with the beans, to make this soup a meal.

2	tablespoons olive oil
4	ounces pancetta, cut into $\frac{1}{4}$-inch pieces
2	medium carrots, peeled and cut into $\frac{1}{2}$-inch pieces
2	celery stalks, thinly sliced
1	onion, diced
3	garlic cloves, halved
1	teaspoon salt, or more to taste
1	teaspoon freshly ground black pepper, or more to taste
2	(14-ounce) cans low-sodium chicken broth
$\frac{1}{2}$	packed cup fresh basil leaves, chopped
2	tablespoons tomato paste
2	teaspoons dried thyme
1	bay leaf
2	bone-in, skin-on chicken breast halves ($1\frac{1}{2}$ to 2 pounds total)
12	ounces frozen artichoke hearts, thawed and chopped into 1-inch pieces
1	(15-ounce) can cannellini beans, rinsed and drained

In a heavy 5- to 6-quart saucepan, heat the oil over medium-high heat. Add the pancetta and cook, stirring frequently, until brown and crispy, 6 to 8 minutes. Using a slotted spoon, remove the pancetta and set aside to drain on paper towels.

Add the carrots, celery, onion, garlic, salt, and pepper to the pan and cook until the onion is translucent, about 5 minutes. Stir in the chicken broth, basil, tomato paste, thyme, and bay leaf. Add the chicken and press to submerge. Bring the liquid to a simmer. Reduce the heat to medium-low and simmer, uncovered, turning the chicken over and stirring occasionally, for 20 minutes.

Add the artichokes and cannellini beans and simmer until the chicken is cooked through and the liquid has reduced slightly, 10 to 15 minutes.

Remove the chicken to a cutting board and let cool for 5 minutes. Discard the skin and bones and cut the meat into bite-size pieces. Return the meat to the saucepan and simmer for 5 minutes, or until warmed through. Discard the bay leaf. Season the spezzatino with salt and pepper, if needed.

To serve, ladle the spezzatino into bowls and garnish with the pancetta.

ligurian fish stew

Liguria is a coastal region in northern Italy known for its fresh seafood and many variations of fish stew, among other things. My version uses just white fish with lots of veggies so it is lighter than many traditional fish stews. It is still sophisticated and is made with white wine, which is a perfect pairing with seafood.

stew

1/3	cup olive oil, plus more for drizzling
2	medium potatoes, peeled and chopped into 3/4-inch pieces
2	medium carrots, peeled and chopped into 1/2-inch pieces
1	onion, chopped
2	garlic cloves, halved
	Salt
3/4	cup dry white wine, such as Pinot Grigio
1	(28-ounce) can crushed Italian San Marzano tomatoes
1/2	teaspoon crushed red pepper flakes, plus more for garnish
1 1/2	pounds skinless white fish fillets, such as halibut, cod, or arctic char, cut into 3/4-inch chunks
1/4	cup chopped fresh flat-leaf parsley leaves

crostini

1	(1-pound) loaf ciabatta bread, trimmed and cut into 14 (1/2-inch-thick) slices
	Olive oil, for drizzling
1	garlic clove, halved

For the stew: In a 6-quart, heavy-bottomed stockpot or Dutch oven, heat the 1/3 cup oil over medium-high heat. Add the potatoes, carrots, onion, and garlic. Season with salt and cook, stirring frequently, until the vegetables begin to soften, 5 to 8 minutes. Turn the heat to high. Add the wine and scrape up the brown bits that cling to the bottom of the pan with a wooden spoon. Cook until most of the liquid has evaporated, about 5 minutes. Add the tomatoes, 1 cup water, and the red pepper flakes. Reduce the heat and bring the mixture to a simmer. Cover and cook until the vegetables are tender, 18 to 20 minutes.

Meanwhile, make the crostini: Place an oven rack in the center of the oven and preheat the oven to 400°F.

Arrange the bread slices in a single layer on a baking sheet and drizzle with olive oil. Bake until light golden, about 10 minutes. Cool for 2 minutes. Rub the warm toasts with the cut side of the garlic.

Season the fish with salt and add to the stew. Cook, stirring occasionally, until cooked through, 5 to 8 minutes.

Season the stew with salt, to taste. Ladle the stew into bowls and garnish with parsley. Drizzle with olive oil and sprinkle a few red pepper flakes on top. Serve with the crostini.

white bean
and chicken chili

4 TO 6 SERVINGS

This chili is perfect cold-weather comfort food. I like to make a quick batch
of it for when Todd and I go skiing. Hearty and healthy, it's full of ground
chicken, corn, Swiss chard, and spices that warm up both you and the dish at
the same time.

2	tablespoons olive oil
1	large onion, chopped
4	garlic cloves, minced
2	pounds ground chicken
	Salt
2	tablespoons ground cumin
1	tablespoon fennel seeds
1	tablespoon dried oregano
2	teaspoons chili powder
3	tablespoons all-purpose flour
2	(15-ounce cans) cannellini or other white beans, rinsed and drained
1	bunch (about 1 pound) Swiss chard, stems removed, leaves chopped into 1-inch pieces
1½	cups frozen corn, thawed
4	cups (1 quart) low-sodium chicken broth
¼	teaspoon crushed red pepper flakes
	Freshly ground black pepper
½	cup freshly grated Parmesan cheese
¼	cup chopped fresh flat-leaf parsley leaves

In a large, heavy-bottomed saucepan or Dutch oven, heat the oil over medium-
high heat. Add the onion and cook until translucent, about 5 minutes. Add
the garlic and cook for 30 seconds. Add the ground chicken, 1 teaspoon salt,
the cumin, fennel seeds, oregano, and chili powder. Cook, stirring frequently,
until the chicken is cooked through, about 8 minutes.

Stir the flour into the chicken mixture. Add the beans, Swiss chard, corn, and chicken broth. Bring the mixture to a simmer, scraping up the brown bits that cling to the bottom of the pan with a wooden spoon. Lower the heat and simmer for 55 to 60 minutes, until the liquid has reduced by about half and the chili has thickened. Add the red pepper flakes and simmer for another 10 minutes. Season with salt and pepper.

Ladle the chili into serving bowls. Sprinkle with the Parmesan cheese and chopped parsley.

butternut squash soup
with fontina cheese crostini

I like to serve this hearty soup at Thanksgiving. It has a smooth, silky texture and a beautiful color with a slight peppery flavor from the sage. Serve it with the cheesy Fontina crostini for an elegant meal.

soup

2	tablespoons unsalted butter, at room temperature
2	tablespoons olive oil
1	medium onion, chopped
1	medium carrot, peeled and chopped into $1/2$-inch pieces
3	garlic cloves, minced
$3^1/2$	pounds butternut squash, peeled, seeded, and cut into $3/4$-inch pieces (7 to 8 cups)
6	cups ($1^1/2$ quarts) low-sodium chicken broth
$1/4$	cup chopped fresh sage leaves
	Salt and freshly ground black pepper

crostini

$1/2$	baguette, sliced diagonally into $1/2$-inch-thick slices
	Olive oil, for drizzling
2	tablespoons chopped fresh sage leaves
1	cup (2 ounces) grated Fontina cheese
	Salt

For the soup: In an 8-quart stockpot, melt the butter and heat the oil together over medium-high heat. Add the onion and carrot. Cook, stirring occasionally, for 5 minutes, or until the onion is soft. Add the garlic and cook for 30 seconds, or until aromatic. Add the squash and chicken broth. Bring the mixture to a boil and add the sage. Continue to boil until the vegetables are tender, about 20 minutes.

Meanwhile, make the crostini: Place an oven rack in the center of the oven and preheat the oven to 400°F.

Arrange the bread slices on a baking sheet. Drizzle with olive oil and sprinkle with the sage. Sprinkle the Fontina on top and season with salt. Bake for 6 to 8 minutes, until the cheese has melted and the bread is light golden.

Turn off the heat under the soup pot. Using an immersion blender or regular blender, purée the mixture until smooth and thick. Season with salt and pepper to taste.

To serve, ladle the soup into bowls and garnish with the Fontina crostini.

lemon chicken soup with spaghetti

4 TO 6 SERVINGS

Nothing warms up a cold winter night like chicken soup, especially when there are hearty chunks of chicken and pieces of pasta waiting in the bottom of the bowl. When I came home from the hospital with Jade, friends and family took turns bringing food by for Todd and me. Sandra Tripicchio, who is an invaluable part of putting together my shows and books, made us a big batch of this lemony chicken soup, and it's been a staple in our house ever since. You'll love the way the lemon brightens the soup's flavor.

6	cups (1½ quarts) low-sodium chicken broth
⅓	cup fresh lemon juice (from 2 lemons)
1	bay leaf
1	medium onion, finely diced
2	medium carrots, peeled and sliced ¼ inch thick
1	celery stalk, thinly sliced
1	cup (about 2½ ounces) broken spaghetti (2-inch pieces are perfect) or short pasta
2	cups diced cooked rotisserie chicken, preferably breast meat
1	cup grated Pecorino Romano cheese
¼	cup chopped fresh flat-leaf parsley leaves
	Salt

In a large stockpot, bring the chicken broth, lemon juice, and bay leaf to a boil over medium-high heat. Add the onion, carrots, and celery and bring to a boil. Reduce the heat so the mixture simmers and cook until the vegetables are tender, 6 to 8 minutes.

Add the pasta and cook, stirring occasionally, for 6 to 8 minutes, or until the pasta is tender. Add the chicken and heat through, 2 to 3 minutes.

Discard the bay leaf. Remove the pot from the heat. Stir in the cheese and the parsley. Season with salt, to taste. Ladle the soup into bowls and serve.

grilled vegetable, herb, and goat cheese sandwiches

4 SERVINGS

Oil flavored with sun-dried tomatoes and lots and lots of fresh herbs is the secret to these vegetarian sandwiches; I use it both as a marinade for the grilled veggies and also to moisten the bread. Creamy goat cheese smoothes out the sharp flavor of the tomatoes. This is perfect picnic food, whether you're packing the sandwiches for the beach or as a reward after a long hike.

1	cup oil-packed sun-dried tomatoes, drained
$1/3$	cup olive oil
2	garlic cloves, minced
$1/2$	cup chopped fresh basil leaves
1	tablespoon chopped fresh tarragon leaves
1	tablespoon chopped fresh thyme leaves
$1/2$	teaspoon salt
$1/2$	teaspoon freshly ground black pepper
2	zucchini, ends trimmed, sliced lengthwise $1/4$ inch thick
2	Japanese eggplants, ends trimmed, sliced lengthwise $1/4$ inch thick
1	($12^1/2$-ounce) baguette, sliced in half lengthwise
1	cup (8 ounces) goat cheese, at room temperature
$1^1/2$	cups (2 ounces) baby spinach

Place a grill pan over medium-high heat or preheat a gas or charcoal grill.

Finely chop the sun-dried tomatoes and put them in a bowl. Add the olive oil, garlic, basil, tarragon, thyme, salt, and pepper.

Spoon 2 tablespoons of the tomato mixture into a medium bowl. Add the zucchini and eggplant to the bowl and toss until coated. Grill the vegetables for 3 to 4 minutes on each side, until tender.

While the vegetables are cooking, spread the remaining tomato mixture on the baguette halves. Using a spatula, spread the goat cheese on top. Layer the grilled vegetables on the bottom half of the baguette. Arrange the spinach over the vegetables. Place the top half of the baguette on top of the filling.

To serve, cut the baguette into 4 sandwiches. Serve immediately or wrap in parchment paper and refrigerate for up to 2 hours.

prosciutto & pancetta

Just as the French have charcuterie, Italians have salumi—meats and sausages that have been preserved either by salting, smoking, cooking, air-drying, or a combination of these methods. These techniques have been used for centuries to ensure that meat would survive both long, cold winters, when fresh meat was scarce, and during the heat of summer, when fresh food spoiled quickly. While refrigeration has made fresh meat available year-round, salumi is such a part of Italian culture they're here to stay and, in fact, are growing in popularity as diners learn about the subtleties and nuances of each variety. Much of Italy's cuisine is regional, so of course salumi-making varies from region to region. From beef and veal bresaola to pork and wild boar salame, salumi is a reflection of the region's traditions, and Italian families continue to cure their meats the same way generation after generation.

Prosciutto and pancetta are two of the better known varieties of salumi, and I use both often in my cooking. Prosciutto is air-cured ham made from the pig's hind leg and is a product of the northern regions, where the temperate climate provides lush valleys and grazing land for the pigs. Prosciutto di Parma from the Emilia-Romagna region as well as Prosciutto di San Daniele from Friuli–Venezia Giulia are widely considered to be of the highest quality. The aging process, during which the meat is rubbed with salt (and no other ingredients) to draw out the moisture and then left to age for at least ten months or more, gives the meat a dense, silky texture and a mild pork flavor with a hint of saltiness. Be sure to choose an imported prosciutto; the region of origin should be marked on the rind. And taste several varieties to find one you like best, as flavors vary based on the length of aging and even the feed the pigs ate. The delicate taste of prosciutto is best appreciated when the meat is sliced thinly and served in simple preparations such as with cheeses and crostini or other antipasti (its salinity is a wonderful match for sweet fruits, such as cantaloupe), as a topping for pizzas, or stirred into pasta sauces at the last minute.

Pancetta, like bacon, is made from the pig's belly and is salt-cured; unlike bacon, it is not smoked, so it has a less assertive flavor. Pancetta is treated to a salt rub to draw out moisture, after which the meat is flavored with spices—such as peppercorns, bay leaf, fennel, and garlic—and left to cure in a temperature- and humidity-controlled environment for three to six months. You'll find pancetta in two forms: either pressed in a large slab covered with a thick layer of fat, or rolled into a cylinder and sold in slices. It freezes well, so keep some on hand to flavor sauces, meat dishes, and pastas, or fry it up to add to panini or antipasti.

piadina with fontina and prosciutto

4 TO 6 SERVINGS

Piadini look a lot like pizzas, but because the crust is made without yeast and does not need to rise, they are much quicker and easier to make. Piadini are also cooked on the grill rather than baked in the oven, which gives them a nice, smoky flavor and crunchy crust. While you can top a piadina with anything you like, including tomato sauce and mozzarella, this sauceless combination is very typical of northern Italy, where piadini are especially popular.

3½ cups all-purpose flour, plus more for dusting

½ teaspoon baking soda

Fine sea salt

½ cup (1 stick) unsalted butter, cut into ½-inch pieces, at room temperature

2 tablespoons olive oil

1 (15-ounce) container (2 cups) whole-milk ricotta cheese

2 teaspoons grated lemon zest (from 1 to 2 lemons)

Freshly ground black pepper

3 cups (6 ounces) grated Fontina cheese

4 ounces prosciutto, thinly sliced

1 cup chopped fresh basil leaves

Combine the flour, baking soda, and 1 teaspoon salt in the bowl of an upright mixer fitted with a dough hook attachment. Add the butter and mix on low speed until incorporated, about 2 minutes. With the machine running, slowly add up to ⅔ cup water, until the mixture forms a dough around the hook. Transfer the dough to a lightly floured work surface and knead for 5 minutes, or until smooth. Cut the dough into 4 equal pieces. Form into disk shapes and wrap in plastic wrap. Refrigerate for 30 minutes.

Place a grill pan over medium-high heat or preheat a gas or charcoal grill.

On a lightly floured work surface, roll out each piece of dough into an 8- to 10-inch circle, about ⅛ inch thick. Brush each circle with the olive oil. Grill for 4 minutes on each side. Remove the piadini from the grill and let cool slightly.

Combine the ricotta cheese and lemon zest in a small bowl. Season with salt and pepper. Spread each piadina with ½ cup of the ricotta mixture. Sprinkle the Fontina cheese evenly over the ricotta cheese. Arrange the prosciutto slices on top of the cheeses. Cut each piadina into 8 wedges and transfer to a serving platter. Garnish with the chopped basil.

zucchini and olive pizza

4 TO 6 SERVINGS

In this country pizza is synonymous with tomato sauce and mozzarella cheese. In some parts of Italy, and especially in Rome, where I grew up, sauce and cheese are generally an either-or proposition, as in this veggie-centric version topped with both mozzarella and sharp pecorino but no sauce. I consider this the perfect item for an evening of playing poker (yes, I do like to play poker); it's easy to eat with your hands, and it will satisfy vegetarians and meat-lovers alike because the olives make it meaty and substantial.

	All-purpose flour, for dusting
1	pound pizza dough, thawed if frozen
1	tablespoon olive oil, plus more for drizzling
1	large (8-ounce) zucchini, trimmed and thinly sliced
2	tablespoons chopped fresh oregano leaves
1½	cups (6 ounces) shredded mozzarella cheese
1	cup (2½ ounces) grated Pecorino Romano cheese
½	cup pitted black olives, sliced

Place an oven rack in the lower third of the oven and preheat the oven to 450°F.

On a lightly floured work surface, roll out the dough into a 12-inch circle. Transfer to a baking sheet lined with parchment paper. With a pastry brush, brush the 1 tablespoon olive oil over the dough. Using the tines of a fork, prick the dough all over.

Arrange the zucchini slices in a single layer on top of the dough. Drizzle the zucchini with olive oil. Bake for 18 to 20 minutes, until the edges begin to brown. Sprinkle the pizza with 1 tablespoon of oregano, the cheeses, and the olives. Bake for 5 to 7 minutes, until the cheeses are melted and bubbly.

Sprinkle the pizza with the remaining oregano, cut into wedges, and serve.

chicken burgers with garlic-rosemary mayonnaise

4 SERVINGS

Burger purists often complain that substituting ground chicken or turkey for beef results in a dry, bland burger, but that needn't be the case; these are super juicy and full of flavor. To keep them moist, I mix some of the garlic mayo right into the burgers themselves, then smear a bit more on each bun for good measure. Easy and yummy, yummy, yummy.

garlic-rosemary mayonnaise

1	cup mayonnaise
¼	cup fresh rosemary leaves, chopped
1	garlic clove, minced

burgers

	Vegetable or canola oil, for the grill
1	pound ground chicken
½	teaspoon salt
¼	teaspoon freshly ground black pepper
4	sandwich rolls or burger buns
¼	cup olive oil
1	cup arugula

For the mayonnaise: Mix together the mayonnaise, rosemary, and garlic.

For the burgers: Preheat a gas or charcoal grill or place a grill pan over medium-high heat. Lightly oil the grilling rack or grill pan with vegetable oil.

In a large bowl, combine the chicken, salt, pepper, and half of the mayonnaise mixture. Using clean hands, gently mix the ingredients and form into 4 patties, each about 1 inch thick. Grill for about 7 minutes on each side, until cooked through. Transfer to paper towels and let rest for a few minutes.

Brush the cut side of each roll with the olive oil and 1 teaspoon of the mayonnaise mixture. Grill for 1 to 2 minutes, until slightly golden.

Spread a dollop of the mayonnaise mixture onto the bun tops and bottoms. Top each bottom with a burger, ¼ cup of arugula, and the top half of the bun.

mini italian pub burgers

8 SERVINGS

The burger phenomenon has never really taken hold in Italy, but the flavors in these dainty little sliders would be right at home there. Taleggio is a northern Italian sharp, creamy cheese that keeps the burgers moist and delicious. The heat of the patty melts the cheese and releases the basil's fresh, herby perfume, making for a decidedly elegant burger experience.

Vegetable or canola oil, for the grill

2¼ pounds ground chuck

¾ cup freshly grated Parmesan cheese

½ cup packed fresh flat-leaf parsley leaves, finely chopped

3 garlic cloves, finely chopped

3 tablespoons tomato paste

1½ teaspoons salt

¼ teaspoon freshly ground black pepper

8 small ciabatta rolls, sliced in half

¼ cup olive oil

8 slices (4½ ounces) Taleggio cheese

8 large basil leaves

Place a grill pan over medium-high heat or preheat a gas or charcoal grill. Lightly oil the grill pan or grilling rack with vegetable oil.

In a large bowl, combine the ground chuck, Parmesan cheese, parsley, garlic, tomato paste, salt, and pepper. Using clean hands, gently mix the ingredients and form into 8 patties, each about 1 inch thick and 4 inches in diameter.

Grill the burgers for 3 minutes on each side, until cooked to medium.

Brush the cut side of each roll with the olive oil and toast on the grill for 1 to 2 minutes, until slightly golden.

To serve, put 1 mini burger on the bottom half of each of the rolls. Divide the Taleggio cheese on top of the burgers. Place a basil leaf over the cheese and put the other half of each roll on top.

open-faced tuna sandwiches with arugula and sweet-pickle mayonnaise

4 SERVINGS

These sandwiches are out-of-this-world fantastic! They're my take on a tuna melt, complete with gooey cheddar cheese and a sweet-and-sour mayo, but with plenty of lemony tang and peppery arugula. Be sure to slather it on the bread generously before piling on the tuna steak, greens, and cheese to keep everything moist and delicious.

½	cup mayonnaise
½	cup finely diced sweet pickles (about 2 pickles)
4	(4- to 6-ounce) albacore tuna steaks
	Salt and freshly ground black pepper
¼	cup olive oil, plus more for drizzling
4	teaspoons herbes de Provence
4	slices sharp white cheddar cheese
1	(1-pound) loaf ciabatta bread, halved horizontally (see Cook's Note)
2	cups arugula

In a small bowl, mix together the mayonnaise and sweet pickles. Set aside.

Place a grill pan over medium-high heat or preheat a gas or charcoal grill.

Season the tuna with salt and pepper. Drizzle with olive oil and sprinkle with the herbes de Provence. Grill for 3 to 4 minutes on each side for medium-rare. Place a slice of cheese on each piece of fish during the last minute of grilling.

Using a pastry brush, brush the bottom half of the bread with the ¼ cup olive oil. Cut into 4 pieces, each about 4 inches long and 3 inches wide. Grill, cut side down, for 30 seconds to 1 minute, until toasted and golden.

Spread the grilled bread with the sweet-pickle mayonnaise. Place a tuna steak on top of each piece. Top with the arugula and drizzle with olive oil. Season with salt and pepper and serve.

COOK'S NOTE: Make the leftover top half of the ciabatta into croutons by cutting into 1-inch cubes, drizzling with olive oil, and baking for 10 to 12 minutes in a preheated 375ºF oven. Alternatively, tear the bread into small pieces, allow to dry, and blend in a food processor to make bread crumbs.

caponata panini

There are as many versions of caponata as there are regions of Italy, and all of them are delicious. Its sweet-and-sour flavor is a perfect complement to roasted meat and it also makes a lovely spread for crostini, but I especially like it paired with salty provolone. Though this hearty vegetarian sandwich tastes so indulgent, it's actually quite light and healthy.

4   sourdough demi-baguettes or rolls, halved lengthwise

8   slices provolone cheese, halved

2   cups Caponata (recipe follows)

special equipment

A panini press, indoor grill, or ridged grill pan (see Cook's Note)

Preheat a panini press or indoor grill.

Using a grapefruit spoon, scoop out a 1-inch-wide trough along the cut sides of the baguettes. Place 2 half-slices provolone cheese on each half of the baguettes. Spoon ½ cup caponata on each of the bottom halves of the baguettes. Invert the top halves of the baguettes on top of the caponata. Grill the panini until the cheese melts and the bread is golden and crispy, about 5 minutes.

COOK'S NOTE: If you do not have a panini press or indoor grill, use a ridged grill pan: Preheat the pan, add the sandwiches (in batches, if necessary), and put a weight (such as a brick wrapped in aluminum foil or a heavy cast-iron skillet) on top to press them down. Grill for 2 to 3 minutes to brown the first side, flip the sandwich, replace the weight, and grill for 2 to 3 minutes to brown the other side and finish melting the cheese.

caponata

MAKES 5 CUPS

Leftover caponata will keep, covered in the refrigerator, for up to a week.
Toss with warm pasta; serve on top of meat, chicken, or fish; or simply
serve it with some toasted bread or crostini.

¼	cup olive oil
1	medium onion, chopped
1	celery stalk, chopped
1	medium eggplant, cut into ½-inch cubes
1	red bell pepper, cored, seeded, and cut into ½-inch pieces
1	(14½-ounce) can diced tomatoes with juices
3	tablespoons raisins
½	teaspoon dried oregano
¼	cup red wine vinegar
4	teaspoons sugar
1	tablespoon capers, rinsed and drained
½	teaspoon salt, or more to taste
½	teaspoon freshly ground black pepper, or more to taste

In a large stainless-steel skillet, heat the olive oil over medium-high heat. Add
the onion and cook until translucent, about 3 minutes. Add the celery and
eggplant and cook until soft, 3 to 4 minutes. Add the bell pepper and cook
until crisp-tender, about 5 minutes. Add the tomatoes, raisins, and oregano to
the pan. Simmer over medium-low heat, stirring frequently, until the mixture
thickens, about 20 minutes. Stir in the vinegar, sugar, capers, salt, and pepper.
Season with more salt and pepper, if needed.

pasta & grains

Bucatini All'Amatriciana with Spicy Smoked
   Mozzarella Meatballs ✸

Rigatoni with Creamy Mushroom Sauce ✸

Orecchiette with Greens, Garbanzo Beans, and Ricotta Salata

Penne with Treviso and Goat Cheese

Pasta Ponza ✸

Spaghetti with Beef, Smoked Almonds, and Basil

Fusilli with Spicy Pesto

Spaghetti with Olives and Bread Crumbs ✸

Cheesy Baked Farro ✸

Nonna Luna's Rice ✸

Brown Butter Risotto with Lobster

Gorgonzola and Porcini Mushroom Risotto ✸

Pasta and—more and more these days—nutritious whole grains are as much a fixture on American tables as they are in Italy, and for good reason. Both pasta and grains are satisfying, healthful, and the perfect blank canvas for any seasonal ingredients you might want to add. They can be hearty and filling or light and refreshing, depending on the weather or your mood. But beyond that, pasta may just be the ultimate comfort food, which is why I still love making the traditional dishes Italian families such as mine have enjoyed for generations.

Nothing makes me feel happier or more satisfied than a plate of pasta and meatballs, the pasta a hearty buccatini with amatriciana sauce and the meatballs, stuffed with smoked mozzarella, served on the side in the classic Italian style. Cold winter days positively demand something cheesy and hot from the oven, and for those times nothing is more soothing than a casserole of farro, an Italian grain similar to barley. It's hard to imagine that anything could improve on these time-trusted standards.

When I'm craving something a little lighter, though, my creativity kicks into high gear. Fusilli with Spicy Pesto (page 88) blends an Italian staple with flavors and ingredients borrowed from Mexican cooking for a zesty dish I love to serve with grilled steak. Pasta salads, a uniquely American invention that you will rarely encounter in Italy, are an easy way to create all-in-one meals that work for lunch, dinner, and even picnics. Take my Spaghetti with Beef, Smoked Almonds, and Basil (page 86): it's a great way to serve beef and pasta without making it a heavy meal, just what you want on a warm day and without the fuss.

bucatini all'amatriciana with spicy smoked mozzarella meatballs

4 TO 6 SERVINGS

This dish is a real mouthful—literally! The pancetta-rich sauce and cheesy meatballs are each delicious on their own and make an irresistible combination. For years my aunt Raffy and I have agreed to disagree on the "right" way to make Amatriciana sauce. She starts with whole tomatoes that cook down to a chunkier sauce, and adds a bit of wine as it cooks. I prefer the lighter, smoother texture of a sauce made with crushed tomatoes (which also save a bit of effort) and think it tastes fresher without the wine. Either way, though, this recipe is a keeper that you'll turn to again and again.

sauce

2	tablespoons olive oil
6	ounces pancetta, diced
1	yellow onion, finely chopped
2	garlic cloves, minced
	Pinch of crushed red pepper flakes
1	(14-ounce) can crushed tomatoes
1/2	teaspoon salt, or more to taste
1/2	teaspoon freshly ground black pepper, or more to taste
1/2	cup grated Pecorino Romano cheese

meatballs

1	small onion, grated
3/4	cup chopped fresh flat-leaf parsley leaves
2/3	cup plus 1/4 cup freshly grated Parmesan cheese
1/3	cup Italian-style seasoned dried bread crumbs
1	large egg
2	tablespoons ketchup
3	garlic cloves, minced
1/4	teaspoon crushed red pepper flakes
1	teaspoon salt, or more to taste

½	teaspoon freshly ground black pepper, or more to taste
8	ounces ground beef
8	ounces ground veal
2	ounces smoked mozzarella cheese, cut into 16 (½-inch) cubes
1	pound bucatini or other long pasta

For the sauce: In a large, heavy skillet, heat the oil over medium heat. Add the pancetta and cook, stirring constantly, until golden brown, 5 to 7 minutes. Using a slotted spoon, remove the pancetta and set aside.

Add the onion to the skillet and cook for 5 minutes. Stir in the garlic and red pepper flakes and cook until fragrant, about 30 seconds. Add the tomatoes, salt, black pepper, and the cooked pancetta. Simmer, uncovered, over medium-low heat until the sauce thickens, about 15 minutes. Stir in the Pecorino Romano cheese and season with salt and pepper, if needed.

For the meatballs: Position an oven rack in the lower third of the oven and preheat the oven to 400°F. Line a rimmed baking sheet with parchment paper.

In a large bowl, combine the onion, ½ cup of the parsley, ⅔ cup of the Parmesan cheese, the bread crumbs, egg, ketchup, garlic, red pepper flakes, salt, and pepper. Add the beef and veal. Using your hands, combine the ingredients gently but thoroughly. Shape the meat mixture into 16 1½-inch-diameter meatballs and place on the prepared baking sheet. Make a depression in the center of each meatball and place a cube of mozzarella inside. Re-form the meatball so that the mozzarella is completely covered with the meat mixture.

Bake the meatballs for 15 minutes, or until cooked through.

Meanwhile, bring a large pot of salted water to a boil over high heat. Add the pasta and cook until tender but still firm to the bite, stirring occasionally, 8 to 10 minutes.

Drain the pasta and place in a large serving bowl. Add the sauce. Toss gently and season with salt and pepper, if needed. Sprinkle with the remaining ¼ cup parsley and ¼ cup Parmesan cheese. Put the meatballs in a separate bowl and serve alongside the pasta.

rigatoni with creamy mushroom sauce

4 TO 6 SERVINGS

This dish hails from northern Italy, where the climate is mushroom-happy and cream sauces are the norm. In lean times, frugal Italian cooks often substituted mushrooms for meat in dishes like this one because their meaty texture and earthy flavor give the sauce real substance. I often make this as a veggie option for parties, and even the carnivores go for it.

1   pound rigatoni pasta

2   tablespoons olive oil

2   shallots, minced

1   garlic clove, minced
      Salt and freshly ground black pepper

1   pound assorted mushrooms (such as cremini, shiitake, or button), cleaned and sliced

½   cup dry white wine

½   cup vegetable broth

1   cup (8 ounces) mascarpone cheese, at room temperature

½   cup freshly grated Parmesan cheese

¼   cup chopped fresh chives

Bring a large pot of salted water to a boil over high heat. Add the pasta and cook, stirring occasionally, until tender but still firm to the bite, 8 to 10 minutes.

Meanwhile, heat the oil in a large skillet over medium-high heat. Add the shallots and garlic and season with salt and pepper. Cook until soft, about 2 minutes. Add the mushrooms and season with salt and pepper. Cook, stirring occasionally, until the mushrooms are tender, 5 to 7 minutes. Turn the heat to high. Add the wine and cook for 3 minutes, or until all the liquid evaporates. Add the broth and simmer until the liquid is slightly reduced.

Remove the pan from the heat. Add the mascarpone cheese and stir until creamy. Drain the pasta, reserving about 1 cup of the pasta water, and transfer to a serving bowl. Add the mushroom mixture and the Parmesan. Season with salt and pepper and toss well to coat the pasta, adding the reserved pasta water, if needed, to loosen the pasta. Garnish with the chopped chives.

orecchiette with greens, garbanzo beans, and ricotta salata

4 TO 6 SERVINGS

We should all be eating more dark leafy greens, but sometimes a side dish of steamed chard is a tough sell. Not so with this pasta, which is full of bright colors and flavors. If you're not familiar with ricotta salata, it may remind you of feta cheese but with a milder flavor and creamier texture. This is a pasta dish I really feel good about eating, and with all those greens and the protein contributed by the garbanzos, it's a complete meal.

1	pound orecchiette or other short pasta
$1/2$	cup olive oil
2	garlic cloves, crushed
12	ounces Swiss chard or mustard greens, stemmed and chopped (9 cups)
8	cups (12 ounces) baby spinach leaves
1	(15-ounce) can garbanzo beans, rinsed and drained
2	cups (12 ounces) small cherry or grape tomatoes
2	cups (8 ounces) crumbled ricotta salata cheese
2	teaspoons grated lemon zest (from 1 to 2 lemons)
	Salt and freshly ground black pepper

Bring a large pot of salted water to a boil over high heat. Add the pasta and cook, stirring occasionally, until tender but still firm to the bite, 8 to 10 minutes.

In a large skillet, heat the oil over medium-high heat. Add the garlic and cook until fragrant and lightly browned, about 2 minutes. Using a slotted spoon, remove the garlic and discard. Add the Swiss chard and cook until wilted, about 5 minutes. In batches, add the spinach and cook until wilted, about 5 minutes. Add the beans and tomatoes and cook for 5 minutes. Turn off the heat.

Drain the pasta, reserving about 1 cup of the pasta water. Transfer the pasta to the skillet and add half of the cheese and the lemon zest. Toss well. If needed, thin out the sauce with a little pasta water and season with salt and pepper. Transfer to a large serving bowl. Sprinkle with the remaining cheese and serve.

penne with treviso and goat cheese

4 TO 6 SERVINGS

Treviso is a leafy vegetable found all over northern Italy, especially around Venice. It looks like a cross between romaine lettuce and radicchio, whose burgundy color and slightly bitter flavor it shares. I like to wilt treviso and then add it to pasta with some creamy goat cheese to mellow its bitterness.

1	pound penne pasta
1/4	cup olive oil
1	garlic clove, halved
1	pound treviso (or radicchio), chopped (about 4 cups)
3	packed cups (5 ounces) baby spinach
1/2	cup low-sodium chicken broth
1/4	cup balsamic vinegar
2	tablespoons fresh lemon juice (from 1 lemon)
1/2	teaspoon crushed red pepper flakes
1	tablespoon salt, or more to taste
1 1/2	cups freshly grated Parmesan cheese
1 1/2	cups (12 ounces) goat cheese, crumbled
1/2	cup fresh basil leaves, torn

Bring a large pot of salted water to a boil over high heat. Add the pasta and cook, stirring occasionally, until tender but still firm to the bite, 8 to 10 minutes.

Meanwhile, in a 12-inch skillet, heat the oil over medium heat. Add the garlic and cook until fragrant and golden, about 1 minute. Remove the garlic and discard.

Add the treviso, spinach, chicken broth, balsamic vinegar, lemon juice, red pepper flakes, and salt. Cook until the treviso and spinach wilt, 6 to 8 minutes.

Drain the pasta, reserving about 1 cup of the pasta water. Add the pasta and Parmesan cheese to the skillet. Toss well, thinning out the sauce with a little pasta water, if needed. Season with salt, if needed.

Transfer the penne to serving bowls. Top each portion with the crumbled goat cheese and garnish with basil before serving.

pasta ponza

4 TO 6 SERVINGS

Ponza is an island off the west coast of Italy where my aunt Raffy and I first tasted this dish, in the home of a family friend. Like all the best pasta dishes, this one is simple; what makes it special is how the sauce comes together. The tomatoes and capers are roasted with a bread crumb topping, concentrating their flavors and making them very juicy with a crunchy crust. When they're mixed with the hot pasta and cheese, the textures and flavors explode in your mouth. This just might be my favorite recipe in the book!

Unsalted butter, for greasing

2   cups (12 ounces) red cherry or grape tomatoes, halved

2   cups (12 ounces) yellow cherry or grape tomatoes, halved

1/4   cup capers, rinsed and drained

1   tablespoon olive oil, plus more for drizzling

1/2   teaspoon salt, or more to taste

1/4   teaspoon freshly ground black pepper, or more to taste

1/2   cup Italian-style seasoned dried bread crumbs

1   pound ziti or other short tube-shaped pasta

1 1/4   cups grated Pecorino Romano cheese

1/4   cup chopped fresh flat-leaf parsley leaves

Place an oven rack in the center of the oven and preheat the oven to 375°F. Butter an 8 x 8-inch glass baking dish. Set aside.

Combine the tomatoes, capers, olive oil, salt, and pepper in the prepared baking dish. Toss to coat. Sprinkle the bread crumbs over the tomato mixture. Drizzle the top with olive oil and bake for 30 to 35 minutes, until the top is golden. Cool for 5 minutes.

Meanwhile, bring a large pot of salted water to a boil over high heat. Add the pasta and cook, stirring occasionally, until tender but still firm to the bite, 8 to 10 minutes.

Drain the pasta, reserving about 1 cup of the pasta water. Transfer the pasta to a large serving bowl. Spoon the tomato mixture onto the pasta. Add the cheese and toss well. If needed, thin out the sauce with a little pasta water. Season with salt and pepper, sprinkle with parsley, and serve immediately.

spaghetti with beef, smoked almonds, and basil

4 TO 6 SERVINGS

The sauce for this pasta is really a simple fresh salsa, and if you are making it in the summer months, feel free to substitute two or three diced beefsteak tomatoes for the canned. It is just as good at room temperature as it is served hot, so it can be made ahead of time—perfect for large get-togethers and buffet-style parties. The sliced steak turns this dish into a meal. I'm seeing smoked almonds used more and more in Italy and I have fallen in love with the deep flavor they add; however, as they are quite salty, when I use them in a dish I reduce the amount of salt I would normally add.

1	pound beef tenderloin steaks (see Cook's Note)
	Salt and freshly ground black pepper
2	teaspoons herbes de Provence
1/4	cup olive oil, plus more for drizzling
1	pound spaghetti pasta
1	(15-ounce) can diced tomatoes
2	packed cups fresh basil leaves plus 1/4 cup chopped
1	garlic clove, chopped
1	teaspoon grated lemon zest
2	teaspoons fresh lemon juice
3/4	cup chopped smoked almonds
1/2	cup freshly grated Parmesan cheese

Place an oven rack in the upper third of the oven and preheat the oven to 450°F.

Place the steaks on a rimmed baking sheet and season with salt and pepper. Sprinkle the herbes de Provence on both sides of the steaks and drizzle with olive oil. Roast for 10 to 12 minutes for medium. Let the steaks rest for 10 minutes on a cutting board.

Meanwhile, bring a large pot of salted water to a boil over high heat. Add the pasta and cook, stirring occasionally, until tender but still firm to the bite, 8 to 10 minutes.

In a food processor, combine the tomatoes and their juices with 2 cups basil leaves, the garlic, lemon zest, lemon juice, and the ¼ cup olive oil. Process until the mixture is coarsely chopped.

Drain the pasta, reserving about 1 cup of the pasta water. Transfer the cooked pasta to a large serving bowl. Add the tomato mixture and smoked almonds and toss well. If needed, thin out the sauce with a little pasta water and season with salt and pepper. Garnish with the Parmesan cheese and chopped basil. Slice the steaks ¼ inch thick and serve alongside the pasta.

COOK'S NOTE: You are looking for steaks that are 1 inch thick. If you don't want to turn on the oven, the steaks can be grilled over medium-high heat in a preheated grill pan or on a gas or charcoal grill for about 5 minutes on each side.

fusilli with spicy pesto

4 TO 6 SERVINGS

I don't cook with jalapeño peppers often because I'm not a huge fan of spicy food, but when I was served grilled fish topped with a spicy pesto at a beach-side restaurant near San Diego, I loved the way the heat woke up the flavor of the fish. I thought it could do the same for pasta, and sure enough, it's a great combo. Packed with spinach and arugula, this pesto is more condiment and less sauce than the typical basil pesto, and a bit lighter thanks to the substitution of walnuts for oily pine nuts. Fusilli is the perfect partner for any kind of pesto because the sauce gets trapped in the ridges so you get flavor in every bite. Serve leftovers of the dressed pasta with roasted chicken, fish, or beef.

1	cup chopped walnuts
2	garlic cloves, coarsely chopped
1	(2-inch) red or green jalapeño pepper, stemmed and coarsely chopped (see Cook's Note)
2	cups (78 ounces) grated Asiago cheese plus ½ cup (2 ounces) shaved
2	teaspoons salt, or more to taste
1	teaspoon freshly ground black pepper, or more to taste
2	cups (3 ounces) baby spinach
3	cups (3 ounces) arugula
¼	cup olive oil
1	pound fusilli pasta

In a food processor, combine the walnuts, garlic, jalapeño, grated cheese, salt, and pepper. Process until the mixture is smooth. Add the spinach and arugula and process until blended. With the machine running, gradually add the olive oil.

Bring a large pot of salted water to a boil over high heat. Add the pasta and cook, stirring occasionally, until tender but still firm to the bite, 8 to 10 minutes. Drain the pasta, reserving about 1 cup of the pasta water. Transfer the cooked pasta to a large serving bowl and add the pesto. Toss well. If needed, thin out the sauce with a little pasta water and season with salt and pepper.

Garnish with the Asiago cheese shavings and serve.

COOK'S NOTE: If you prefer a milder pesto, remove the seeds from the jalapeño pepper before you chop it.

spaghetti with olives and bread crumbs

4 TO 6 SERVINGS

Here's a dish that is so much more than the sum of its parts, which are all simple pantry ingredients that you probably have on hand right now. Bread crumbs were traditionally a thrifty way for Italian housewives to use up leftover crusts of bread, but they really make the dish; sautéed in olive oil, the bread crumbs get crispy and make a crunchy crust on each strand of pasta. I use black and green olives to get both the fruity and the salty flavors, but if you have only one or the other the dish will still be great. It really doesn't get much easier than this—or more appealing.

1	pound spaghetti pasta
3/4	cup olive oil
2/3	cup Italian-style seasoned dried bread crumbs
1/4	teaspoon salt, or more to taste
1/4	teaspoon freshly ground black pepper, or more to taste
3/4	cup pitted and coarsely chopped black olives, such as kalamata
3/4	cup pitted and coarsely chopped large green olives, such as Cerignola
1/3	cup freshly grated Parmesan cheese
4	tablespoons chopped fresh flat-leaf parsley leaves

Bring a large pot of salted water to a boil. Add the pasta and cook, stirring occasionally, until tender but still firm to the bite, about 8 minutes.

Meanwhile, in a large sauté pan, heat the oil over medium-high heat. Add the bread crumbs, salt, and pepper. Stirring constantly, cook the bread crumbs until golden brown, about 2 minutes.

Drain the pasta, reserving 1 cup of the pasta water. Stir the pasta into the bread crumb mixture. Remove the pan from the heat and add the black and green olives. Add the Parmesan cheese and 3 tablespoons of the parsley. Season the pasta with salt and pepper, if needed. Gently toss to coat, adding reserved pasta water, if needed, to loosen the pasta. Transfer to a large serving bowl and garnish with the remaining 1 tablespoon parsley.

cheesy baked farro

We think of mac and cheese as a true-blue American invention, but this homey dish, made with nutty farro, is actually very traditional. Farro is one of the first cultivated grains and was ground to make bread, cereals, and pasta in ancient Italy. It's becoming more popular in this country, but you still may need to visit an Italian specialty store to find it. Use it in salads, pilafs, and soups as you would use barley, which is also a good substitute for farro.

Vegetable oil cooking spray

sauce

4	tablespoons (1/2 stick) unsalted butter
1/4	cup all-purpose flour
2	cups warm milk
	Salt and freshly ground black pepper

farro

6	cups (1 1/2 quarts) low-sodium chicken broth
2	cups farro, rinsed and drained
2	tablespoons olive oil, plus more for drizzling
2	cups assorted mushrooms (such as button, cremini, or portobello), cleaned and sliced
	Salt and freshly ground black pepper
3/4	cup halved cherry or grape tomatoes
2 1/2	cups freshly grated Parmesan cheese
1	cup (4 ounces) grated Gruyère cheese
1/2	cup (about 1 ounce) grated Fontina cheese
1	teaspoon chopped fresh thyme leaves
1/2	cup plain dried bread crumbs

Preheat the oven to 400°F. Spray a 9 x 13-inch baking dish with cooking spray.

For the sauce: In a 2-quart saucepan, melt the butter over medium heat. Add the flour and whisk until smooth. Gradually add the warm milk, whisking

recipe continues

constantly to prevent lumps. Simmer over medium heat, whisking constantly, until the sauce is thick and smooth, about 8 minutes (do not allow the mixture to boil). Remove from the heat and season with salt and pepper.

For the farro: In an 8-quart stockpot, bring the chicken broth to a boil over medium-high heat. Add the farro, lower the heat, and simmer, stirring occasionally, until tender, about 25 minutes. Drain if necessary.

In a large skillet, heat the oil over medium-high heat. Add the mushrooms and season with salt and pepper. Cook the mushrooms, stirring occasionally, for 8 minutes or until tender. Add the tomatoes to the pan and cook for 2 to 3 minutes, until tender.

In a large bowl, combine the Parmesan cheese, Gruyère cheese, Fontina cheese, and thyme. Remove ½ cup of the mixture and set aside. Add the cooked farro, sauce, and mushroom mixture to the cheeses. Stir until combined. Season with salt and pepper. Pour the mixture into the prepared baking dish and sprinkle with the ½ cup reserved cheese mixture. Sprinkle the top with bread crumbs and drizzle with olive oil.

Bake until the top is golden brown and forms a crust, 25 to 30 minutes. Remove from the oven and let stand for 5 minutes before serving.

nonna luna's rice

4 SERVINGS

Italy is best known for its short-grain rice dishes, like risotto, but long-grain rice is popular there as well. My grandmother Nonna Luna loved to cook rice, and her secret was toasting the grains before adding the broth and a tablespoon of hot sauce. Unlike in a risotto, the grains stay fluffy and separate, not starchy. This dish is super easy to make—the only trick is taking the full six to seven minutes needed to toast the rice grains. That step gives the dish a nutty flavor that takes it from good to great, and the shrimp make it a full meal.

½ cup (1 stick) unsalted butter, at room temperature

2 cups parboiled long-grain rice, such as Uncle Ben's

3½ cups low-sodium chicken broth

2 tablespoons hot sauce, such as Tabasco

Salt

1 garlic clove

2 pounds small shrimp, peeled and deveined

½ cup fresh lemon juice (from 2 to 3 lemons)

1 cup heavy cream

Freshly ground black pepper

In a medium nonstick saucepan, heat half of the butter over medium-low heat. Add the rice and cook, stirring frequently, until golden, 6 to 7 minutes. Add the chicken broth, 1 tablespoon of the hot sauce, and 2 teaspoons salt. Bring the mixture to a boil over medium-high heat. Reduce the heat to medium-low and simmer, covered, for 20 to 25 minutes, until the rice is tender and all the liquid is absorbed. Remove the pan from the heat and let rest, covered, for 5 minutes.

In a large skillet, melt the remaining butter over medium heat. Add the garlic and cook, stirring frequently, for 1 to 2 minutes, until aromatic. Add the shrimp, lemon juice, and remaining 1 tablespoon hot sauce. Cook for 2 to 3 minutes, until the shrimp are pink and cooked through. Stir in the cream and heat through. Season with salt and pepper.

Using a fork, fluff the rice and scoop out onto a platter. Spoon the shrimp cream sauce over the rice and serve.

brown butter risotto
with lobster

4 SERVINGS

This dish has become very popular on restaurant menus, because it seems extra-special—and tricky to make at home. Special it is, but in fact it's quite easy to pull off, as it uses frozen lobster tails—no live lobsters to boil. The key is to brown the butter well for a deep, nutty flavor.

1	pound (about 2 medium) frozen lobster tails, thawed
4½	cups low-sodium chicken broth
4	tablespoons (½ stick) unsalted butter, at room temperature
1	medium onion, finely chopped
1½	cups Arborio rice
½	cup brandy
½	cup freshly grated Parmesan cheese
¼	cup chopped fresh chives
	Salt and freshly ground black pepper

Bring a medium saucepan of salted water to a boil over medium-high heat. Add the lobster tails and boil for 8 to 10 minutes, until the meat turns white. Drain and cool for 15 minutes. Using a sharp knife, cut through the top shell lengthwise. Remove the meat and cut into ½-inch pieces. Set aside.

In a saucepan, bring the chicken broth to a boil. Keep hot over low heat.

In a large saucepan, melt 3 tablespoons of the butter over medium heat. Cook until the butter begins to foam and brown, 1 to 1½ minutes. Add the onion and cook until tender, about 3 minutes. Add the rice and stir to coat. Add the brandy and simmer until the liquid has almost evaporated, about 3 minutes.

Add ½ cup of the broth and stir until almost completely absorbed, about 2 minutes. Continue adding the broth, ½ cup at a time, stirring constantly and allowing each addition of broth to absorb before adding the next. Cook until the rice is tender but still firm to the bite, about 20 minutes in total. Remove from the heat. Stir in the Parmesan cheese, the remaining 1 tablespoon butter, and half of the chives. Season with salt and pepper.

Transfer the risotto to a large serving bowl. Arrange the lobster meat on top of the risotto and garnish with the remaining chives.

gorgonzola and porcini mushroom risotto

4 TO 6 SERVINGS

This is a dish typically found in the Lombardy region of Italy, or in the Veneto. The extra-creamy consistency of this risotto belies its bold flavors: each super-rich bite is woodsy and earthy all in one. Because it's so rich, a small portion makes a big impact. I serve it with a simple side salad and a full-bodied red wine, such as a Barbera.

4	cups (1 quart) low-sodium chicken broth
1½	ounces dried porcini mushrooms
3	tablespoons unsalted butter
1	medium onion, finely chopped
1½	cups Arborio rice
½	cup dry white wine
½	cup freshly grated Parmesan cheese
¾	cup (3 ounces) crumbled Gorgonzola cheese
¼	cup chopped fresh chives
½	teaspoon salt
¼	teaspoon freshly ground black pepper

In a medium saucepan, bring the broth to a boil over medium-high heat. Add the porcini mushrooms. Remove the pan from the heat and set aside for 30 minutes. Using a slotted spoon, remove the mushrooms and set aside.

Reheat the broth to a simmer and keep hot over low heat.

In a large, heavy saucepan, melt 2 tablespoons of the butter over medium-high heat. Add the onion and mushrooms and cook until the onion is tender but not brown, about 3 minutes. Add the rice and stir to coat with the butter. Add the wine and simmer until the wine has almost evaporated, about 3 minutes.

Add ½ cup of the broth and stir until almost completely absorbed, about 2 minutes. Continue adding broth, ½ cup at a time, stirring constantly, and allowing each addition to be absorbed, until the rice is tender but still firm to the bite and the mixture is creamy, about 20 minutes in total.

Remove the pan from the heat. Stir in the Parmesan, Gorgonzola, chives, salt, and pepper. Transfer the risotto to a serving bowl. Serve immediately.

meat,
poultry
& fish

Steak Involtini ❀

Grilled Tuscan Steak with Fried Egg and Goat Cheese ❀

Roasted Beef Tenderloin with Basil-Curry Mayonnaise

Chianti Marinated Beef Stew ❀

Chicken Milanese with Tomato and Fennel Sauce ❀

Chicken and Shrimp with Pancetta Chimichurri

Turkey Meatloaf with Feta and Sun-Dried Tomatoes

Roasted Citrus-Herb Game Hens with Crouton Salad

Honey-Balsamic Lamb Chops ❀

Honey-Mustard Pork Roast with Bacon

Roasted Branzino with Lemons ❀

Red Snapper with Fava Bean Purée ❀

Grilled Salmon with Citrus Salsa Verde

Roasted Halibut with Pea and Mint Salad

One of the primary differences between the way Italians have traditionally eaten and how we eat in this country is the role meat plays in the meal. I'm married to a Midwestern guy with a robust appetite, and like many Americans, Todd likes to see a healthy serving of protein front and center on his plate; the other elements of the meal are definitely supporting players. Italians, on the other hand, go for more of an ensemble approach, allowing pasta, veggies, and other parts of the meal their own moments in the spotlight. In my home we take a hybrid approach that I think draws from the best of both worlds.

Oftentimes it's the occasion that dictates the meal. For large gatherings and holidays, I like to serve a dish that makes a big impression and can be portioned at the table, such as Roasted Beef Tenderloin with Basil-Curry Mayonnaise (page 109) or Honey-Mustard Pork Roast with Bacon (page 126). In other instances, as on Christmas Eve or even in the summer when ingredients are fresh, I'm more likely to roast a whole fish, as they do in southern Italy. Roasting a fish whole keeps it moist and juicy and the flesh is infused with flavor from herbs and lemon tucked in the cavity.

When it's just the two of us I reach for dishes that are quick to cook and have lots of bright flavors. Todd (and most men I know) loves a good steak, and while there are plenty of nights when we simply throw one on the grill, at other times I like to serve steak the way I had it when I was a child, as involtini stuffed with cheese and rolled; as part of a sexy salad; or topped with an egg as in my Grilled Tuscan Steak with Fried Egg and Goat Cheese (page 106).

That said, like many families, we're eating less red meat these days, and I've adapted some favorite dishes to be a bit lighter in taste (and calories) by substituting chicken or turkey for beef. My meatloaf is a great example, packed with feta and sun-dried tomatoes that provide beautiful color in each slice. And we do try to eat fish as often as we can; one purely California-inspired favorite is Grilled Salmon with Citrus Salsa Verde (page 132). It's rich and light and sweet and tangy all in one bite.

steak involtini

4 SERVINGS

Other than in Tuscany, where the thick-cut steak *fiorentina* reigns supreme, you won't find a lot of simple grilled steaks in Italy. Instead, Italians tend to serve their beef pounded thin and braised in a flavorful sauce. Pounding is a good way to tenderize a tougher (and less expensive) cut of beef such as London broil, and the cheesy stuffing here adds lots of flavor. Plus, I find that everyone, especially kids, enjoys the surprise of discovering the rich, melted filling inside these cute little breaded rolls. I know I did when I was a kid . . . and I still do!

- 1 cup plain dried bread crumbs
- 1 cup freshly grated Parmesan cheese
- 3/4 cup shredded mozzarella cheese
- 1/2 cup olive oil
- 1/2 cup chopped fresh basil leaves
- 2 garlic cloves, minced
  Salt and freshly ground black pepper
- 2 (8-ounce) London broil steaks, trimmed and pounded to 1/8 inch thick
- 1 (26-ounce) jar marinara sauce (3 1/3 cups)

special equipment

- 4 (4-inch) skewers

In a small bowl, combine the bread crumbs and ¼ cup of the Parmesan cheese.

In a large bowl, mix together the remaining ¾ cup Parmesan cheese, the mozzarella cheese, ¼ cup of the olive oil, the basil, and garlic to make the filling. Season with salt and pepper. Cut the steaks in half crosswise and place on a work surface. Spread the filling evenly over the steaks. Roll up the steaks and secure with skewers.

In a medium skillet, heat the remaining ¼ cup oil over medium. Roll the steaks in the bread-crumb mixture to coat. Cook the steaks until brown on all sides, 6 to 8 minutes. Add the marinara sauce to the pan and bring to a simmer, scraping up the brown bits from to the bottom of the pan with a wooden spoon. Simmer, turning occasionally, for 10 to 15 minutes for medium-well.

Remove the skewers and slice the meat. Arrange the steak slices on plates and serve with the marinara sauce.

grilled tuscan steak with fried egg and goat cheese

4 SERVINGS

In Italy, as in this country, steak and eggs are a classic combination. But while you'll most often find the dish on breakfast menus here, Italians would be more likely to eat it at lunchtime, their most substantial meal of the day. I remember Todd flipping for it when he first tried it many years ago at my uncle's house in Rome, and now it's one of our favorite easy dinner recipes. Sometimes I serve the steak on a bed of greens, such as arugula, and serve slices of rustic bread alongside to sop up the runny yolk and meat juices. Steak, salad, egg, and bread—what more could you want, any time of day?

4	(8-ounce) rib-eye steaks
	Salt and freshly ground black pepper
2	tablespoons herbes de Provence
2	tablespoons plus 2 teaspoons olive oil
4	large eggs
¼	cup (2 ounces) crumbled goat cheese
2	tablespoons chopped fresh flat-leaf parsley leaves

Place a grill pan over medium-high heat or preheat a gas or charcoal grill.

Season the steaks with salt and pepper. Sprinkle both sides of each steak with the herbes de Provence. Drizzle with 2 tablespoons of the olive oil. Grill for 6 to 8 minutes per side for medium-rare. Remove the steaks from the heat and allow to rest.

Meanwhile, in a medium skillet, heat the remaining 2 teaspoons olive oil over medium-high heat. Crack the eggs directly into the pan and season them with salt and pepper. Cook until the egg whites are set, 2 to 3 minutes.

To serve, place the steaks on 4 serving plates. Carefully top each steak with an egg. Sprinkle with the crumbled goat cheese. Garnish with the chopped parsley and serve.

roasted beef tenderloin with basil-curry mayonnaise

6 TO 8 SERVINGS

You can't really go wrong with a beef tenderloin. It's a prime cut of meat that can be pricey, but I consider it for the holidays and special occasions. Really, it's so tender and flavorful that you don't have to do too much to make it taste delicious. The crust on this tenderloin, with garlic paste, cumin, and coriander, is so simple yet a wonderful surprise, and the basil-curry mayo is perfectly herby, spicy, and creamy. With any leftovers, you can make some pretty gourmet sandwiches, too.

beef

Vegetable oil cooking spray

2 teaspoons cumin seeds

2 teaspoons coriander seeds

3 garlic cloves, peeled

2¼ teaspoons salt

1 teaspoon freshly ground black pepper

2 tablespoons olive oil

1 (3½- to 4-pound) beef tenderloin, trimmed

mayonnaise

1 cup mayonnaise

¼ cup (2 ounces) mascarpone cheese, at room temperature

⅓ cup finely chopped fresh basil leaves

1 tablespoon curry powder

1 teaspoon smoked paprika

Salt and freshly ground black pepper

For the beef: Place an oven rack in the center of the oven and preheat the oven to 400°F. Spray a heavy rimmed baking sheet with vegetable oil cooking spray. Set aside.

recipe continues

In a mortar and pestle or spice grinder, coarsely grind the cumin seeds and coriander seeds (see Cook's Note). Heat a small skillet over medium heat. Add the spices and cook, stirring, for 30 seconds, or until aromatic and toasted. Scrape the spices into a small bowl.

Finely chop the garlic on a cutting board. Sprinkle with ¼ teaspoon of the salt. Holding a chef's knife at a 45-degree angle, scrape the garlic and salt together to form a paste. Spoon the garlic paste into the bowl with the spices. Add the remaining 2 teaspoons salt, the black pepper, and the oil. Stir until smooth.

Place the meat on the prepared baking sheet and rub with the spice mixture. Roast for 35 to 40 minutes, or until a meat thermometer inserted into the thickest part of the meat registers 125°F for medium-rare. Transfer the meat to a cutting board and tent loosely with foil. Let rest for 20 minutes.

For the mayonnaise: In a small bowl, whisk together the mayonnaise, mascarpone cheese, basil, curry powder, and paprika until smooth. Season with salt and pepper.

To serve, slice the meat into ¼-inch-thick slices and arrange on a platter. Spoon the curry mayonnaise into a small bowl and serve alongside the meat.

COOK'S NOTE: You can also crush the spices by putting them in a small resealable plastic bag and pressing down on them with a rolling pin or the bottom of a small saucepan.

chianti marinated beef stew

4 TO 6 SERVINGS

This homey one-pot meal is reminiscent of the stews you find in Tuscany and Umbria, which are loaded with vegetables, potatoes, and herbs. It's a great choice if you're looking for a dish to serve to a crowd; the succulent stew can simmer for a long time—the sauce just becomes richer and more intense—and it's hard to believe you can get so much flavor from a relatively inexpensive piece of meat. Just be sure to use a Chianti that's good enough to serve along with the meal.

1	(2½- to 3-pound) beef brisket
1	(750 ml) bottle Chianti wine
4	tablespoons olive oil
	Salt and freshly ground black pepper
4	ounces pancetta, cut into ¼-inch pieces
3	medium carrots, peeled and cut into ½-inch pieces
1	celery stalk, chopped into ½-inch pieces
2	garlic cloves, peeled
¼	cup kalamata olives, halved
6	ounces green beans, halved
4	medium red potatoes, quartered
2	sprigs fresh rosemary
2	fresh sage leaves
1	(15-ounce) can diced tomatoes
4	cups (1 quart) low-sodium beef broth

Place the beef in a 13 x 9-inch glass baking dish. Pour the wine over the meat and marinate in the refrigerator for 3 hours, turning once halfway through.

Remove the meat from the wine and pat dry with paper towels. Reserve the wine.

In a large Dutch oven, heat 3 tablespoons of the oil over medium-high heat. Season the meat on all sides with salt and pepper. Add the meat to the pan and brown on all sides, about 2 minutes per side. Remove the meat to a plate.

recipe continues

Add the remaining 1 tablespoon oil and the pancetta to the Dutch oven. Cook, stirring frequently, for 2 minutes. Add the carrots, celery, garlic, olives, green beans, potatoes, rosemary, and sage. Cook for 3 minutes. Pour the reserved wine, tomatoes, and beef broth into the pan, scraping up the brown bits that cling to the bottom of the pan with a wooden spoon. Return the meat to the pan and bring the liquid to a boil. Cover the pan and simmer over low heat for 3 to 3½ hours, or until the meat is very tender.

Remove the meat and the rosemary and sage from the stew. Put the meat on a cutting board and cut into quarters. Using 2 forks, shred the meat into bite-size pieces. Add the shredded meat to the stew and heat to warm through before serving, about 5 minutes.

chicken milanese with tomato and fennel sauce

4 TO 6 SERVINGS

Cutlets cooked *à la milanese*—breaded in a cheesy crumb coating and pan-fried until crisp—are popular in every part of Italy (and here, for that matter!). They are usually made with veal, but my little aunt Carolyna wanted something she could serve her college friends, many of whom don't eat veal. So I substituted chicken for the veal and added fennel to the quick pan sauce in this dish I devised for her; it is quite light and fresh-tasting, yet still true to the original.

chicken

1/3	cup all-purpose flour
2	large eggs
1 1/4	cups plain dried bread crumbs
2/3	cup freshly grated Parmesan cheese
2	teaspoons dried basil
1	teaspoon dried thyme
4	(6- to 8-ounce) boneless, skinless chicken breast halves, tenderloins removed
	Salt and freshly ground black pepper
1/3	cup vegetable oil

sauce

1	tablespoon olive oil
2	fennel bulbs, trimmed and thinly sliced, fronds reserved for garnish
2	cups (12 ounces) cherry tomatoes, halved
1	garlic clove, minced
1	teaspoon dried thyme or 1 tablespoon chopped fresh thyme leaves
1/4	teaspoon salt, or more to taste
1/4	teaspoon freshly ground black pepper, or more to taste
1/2	cup (4 ounces) mascarpone cheese, at room temperature

recipe continues

For the chicken: Place an oven rack in the center of the oven and preheat the oven to 150°F. Line a rimmed baking sheet with a wire rack.

Spoon the flour into a wide, shallow bowl. Crack the eggs into another wide, shallow bowl; lightly beat them. In a third wide, shallow bowl, combine the bread crumbs, Parmesan cheese, basil, and thyme.

On a work surface, place the chicken between 2 pieces of plastic wrap. Using a meat mallet, lightly pound the chicken until approximately ¼ to ½ inch thick. Season the chicken with salt and pepper. Dredge the chicken pieces in the flour to coat lightly, then dip into the beaten eggs, allowing the excess egg to drip off. Coat the chicken with the bread-crumb mixture, pressing gently to adhere.

In a large, nonstick sauté pan, heat the vegetable oil over medium heat. Place 2 pieces of breaded chicken in the oil and cook until light golden brown, 3 to 4 minutes on each side. Transfer the chicken to the prepared baking sheet and keep warm in the oven. Repeat with the remaining chicken. Reserve the cooking juices in the pan.

For the sauce: Add the olive oil to the reserved cooking juices in the sauté pan and heat over medium heat. Add the fennel and cook, stirring frequently, until softened, 5 to 6 minutes. Add the cherry tomatoes, garlic, thyme, salt, and pepper. Cook for 5 to 6 minutes, until the tomatoes are tender. Remove the pan from the heat. Add the mascarpone cheese and stir until the mixture is creamy. Season with salt and pepper, if needed.

To serve, arrange the chicken on a serving platter and spoon the sauce on top. Garnish with the fennel fronds.

dried vs.
fresh herbs

I love freshly picked herbs. There's nothing quite as aromatic and satisfying, and I use them as much as possible. You can put them in most any dish, and they are especially desirable in salads, pastas, pestos, and sauces. They're also pretty as a garnish.

But dried herbs have their place, too.

Because they are picked at their peak of flavor (just before flowering), dried herbs have a highly concentrated flavor; when the moisture is extracted from the leaves, the potent herb oils remain. For braising, stewing, or other dishes with long cooking times and lots of liquid, dried herbs are a good option, as they won't burn or discolor. They pack a more powerful punch than fresh herbs, whose flavors are subtler and tend to dissipate with long cooking.

Dried herbs have a shelf life of anywhere from six months to one year. Buy dried herbs that appear deep green, not faded. And always smell your herbs before you use them; if they smell musty or don't smell much at all, it's time to replace them.

In many recipes dried herbs can be substituted for fresh and vice versa. The general rule is to use three times as much fresh herb as you would use of the dried form; if substituting dried for fresh, use just one-third of the quantity called for.

chicken and shrimp with pancetta chimichurri

6 TO 8 SERVINGS

Chimichurri is the A1 sauce of Argentina, and no self-respecting steak there would be served without a dose of this herby green sauce. But chimichurri also has a lot in common with an Italian salsa verde, which gave me the idea to pair it with the more delicate combo of chicken and shrimp. I add oregano for a deep earthiness, and crunchy bites of pancetta put it over the top; you'll want to serve this sauce over everything from broiled fish fillets to sliced tomatoes or even crostini.

chimichurri

2	tablespoons plus 1 cup olive oil
8	ounces pancetta, cut into ¼-inch dice
3	garlic cloves
1	cup packed fresh flat-leaf parsley leaves
½	cup fresh oregano leaves or 2 tablespoons dried
⅓	cup red wine vinegar
3	tablespoons fresh lemon juice (from 1 lemon)
	Salt and freshly ground black pepper

chicken and shrimp

6	(6-ounce) boneless, skinless chicken breast halves
1	pound jumbo shrimp, peeled and deveined
2	tablespoons dried oregano
	Salt and freshly ground black pepper
	Olive oil, for drizzling

For the chimichurri: In a small skillet, heat 2 tablespoons of the olive oil over medium-high heat. Add the pancetta and cook, stirring constantly, until browned, 6 to 8 minutes. Drain on paper towels. Set aside.

In the bowl of a food processor, combine the garlic, parsley, oregano, vinegar, remaining 1 cup olive oil, and the lemon juice. Pulse until smooth. Season with salt and pepper.

For the chicken and shrimp: Preheat a grill pan or a gas or charcoal grill.

Season the chicken and shrimp with the dried oregano and salt and pepper. Drizzle with olive oil. Grill the chicken for 5 to 6 minutes on each side, until cooked through. Grill the shrimp for 1 to 2 minutes on each side, until pink and cooked through.

Slice the chicken diagonally and arrange on a large serving platter with the shrimp. Drizzle with the chimichurri and sprinkle with the pancetta.

turkey meatloaf with feta and sun-dried tomatoes

4 SERVINGS

I like to make turkey meatloaf as a way to serve up a satisfying meaty entrée without resorting to red meat. I load it with sweet sun-dried tomatoes and salty bites of feta, which just barely melt as the meatloaf bakes. When you cut into the meatloaf it looks so colorful. This is one of my top picks for serving a large group because it makes a lot, is hearty, and doesn't require any last-minute fussing. Leftovers make terrific sandwiches the next day, too.

Vegetable oil cooking spray

½	cup plain dried bread crumbs
⅓	cup chopped fresh flat-leaf parsley leaves
¼	cup chopped garlic- and herb-marinated sun-dried tomatoes
2	garlic cloves, minced
2	large eggs, at room temperature, lightly beaten
¼	cup olive oil
½	cup crumbled feta cheese
1½	teaspoons salt
1	teaspoon freshly ground black pepper
1	pound ground turkey, preferably dark meat

Place an oven rack in the center of the oven and preheat the oven to 350°F. Spray a 9 x 5-inch nonstick loaf pan with cooking spray.

In a large bowl, stir together the bread crumbs, parsley, sun-dried tomatoes, garlic, eggs, olive oil, feta, salt, and pepper. Add the turkey and gently stir to combine, being careful not to overwork the meat. Carefully pack the meat mixture into the prepared pan; it will fill the pan halfway. Bake until the internal temperature registers 165°F on an instant-read thermometer, 40 to 45 minutes.

Remove the pan from the oven and let the meatloaf rest for 5 minutes. Use a paper towel to remove any fat that may settle on the surface of the meatloaf. Slice and serve.

roasted citrus-herb game hens with crouton salad

2 SERVINGS

Few things are more enticing than the smell of a chicken roasting, but for a special meal or a romantic evening such as Valentine's Day, I like to serve game hens, so each person can have a whole bird of his or her own. It's a beautiful presentation that is ridiculously easy to put together, and the pan juices, full of fresh citrus flavors, are especially delicious. If you prefer, though, you can easily make this with a large chicken; just increase the roasting time to 60 to 75 minutes, depending on its weight.

crouton salad

$\frac{1}{2}$	(8-ounce) loaf of rosemary, olive, or plain rustic bread, cut into $\frac{1}{2}$-inch cubes
$\frac{1}{3}$	cup pine nuts
3	packed cups (3 ounces) arugula
	Salt and freshly ground black pepper

game hens

2	(1$\frac{1}{2}$- to 2-pound) Cornish game hens
$\frac{1}{4}$	cup olive oil
2	shallots, minced
2	tablespoons grated orange zest (from 2 medium oranges)
2	tablespoons grated lemon zest (from about 3 lemons)
2	tablespoons chopped fresh thyme leaves
3	tablespoons chopped fresh mint leaves
	Salt and freshly ground black pepper
2	cups low-sodium chicken broth
2	tablespoons Marsala wine or dry sherry
2	tablespoons fresh lemon juice (from 1 lemon)
2	tablespoons fresh orange juice
$\frac{1}{4}$	cup dried cranberries or currants
2	teaspoons all-purpose flour
2	tablespoons unsalted butter, at room temperature

recipe continues

For the crouton salad: Place an oven rack in the lower third of the oven and preheat the oven to 350°F.

Scatter the bread cubes on a rimmed baking sheet and bake for 12 to 15 minutes, until toasted. Set aside to cool.

Meanwhile, heat a small, heavy skillet over medium-low heat. Add the pine nuts to the hot skillet and stir them until they become fragrant and golden brown, about 5 minutes. Transfer to a plate to cool.

For the game hens: Increase the oven temperature to 450°F.

Rinse the game hens and pat dry with paper towels. In a small bowl, mix together the olive oil, shallots, orange zest, lemon zest, thyme, mint, 1 teaspoon salt, and 1 teaspoon pepper. Rub 2 tablespoons of the zest mixture over the skins of the game hens. Work the remainder of the zest mixture under the skin and into the cavities of the hens. Using kitchen twine, tie the legs together. Place the hens in a shallow 9 x 13-inch baking dish. Add the chicken broth, Marsala wine, lemon juice, orange juice, and cranberries. Roast for 30 to 35 minutes, or until the game hens are browned and the leg juices run clear when the legs are pierced with a knife.

Remove the game hens from the pan and set aside. Spoon the flour into a small saucepan. Whisk in the pan juices from the baking dish. Bring the juices to a boil over medium heat. Reduce the heat and simmer for 8 to 10 minutes, until slightly thickened. Whisk in the butter and season the sauce with salt and pepper.

In a medium salad bowl, mix together the cooled croutons, pine nuts, and arugula. Add ¼ cup of the pan sauce. Toss well until all the ingredients are coated. Season with salt and pepper.

To serve, remove the kitchen twine from the game hens and place the hens on 2 serving plates. Serve with the salad and drizzle with the remaining sauce.

honey-balsamic lamb chops

4 TO 6 SERVINGS

In my experience even people who complain that lamb can taste too gamey love lamb chops. I would be lying if I didn't also acknowledge that lamb chops are the most expensive cut, but I think they're worth it, because they deliver a lot of flavor in just minutes. These chops, with a sweet tangy dressing drizzled on top, are an easy and fast meal that delivers, specifically on special occasions or for a Sunday night family dinner. Even Jade loves them!

⅓	cup balsamic vinegar
1	garlic clove, peeled
2	tablespoons honey
¾	cup vegetable or canola oil
	Salt and freshly ground black pepper
8	small lamb chops
2	tablespoons olive oil
½	tablespoon chopped fresh rosemary leaves

Place a grill pan over medium-high heat or preheat a gas or charcoal grill.

In the bowl of a food processor, combine the balsamic vinegar, garlic, and honey. Pulse until blended. With the machine running, slowly pour in the vegetable oil and process until the mixture is smooth and forms a thick sauce. Season with salt and pepper.

Season the lamb chops with salt and pepper. Drizzle with the olive oil and sprinkle with the rosemary. Grill the lamb chops for 2 to 3 minutes on each side for medium-rare.

Arrange the lamb chops on a platter. Spoon the sauce over the top or serve it on the side.

honey-mustard pork roast with bacon

6 SERVINGS

I recently served this roast for the Thanksgiving holiday, thinking a departure from the usual turkey would be a welcome surprise—and it definitely was. The sweetness from the mustards absorbs into the meat, while the bacon keeps it nice and moist and adds a wonderful smokiness. Served over a lightly dressed fresh arugula salad, this will become a fast favorite—I promise.

roast

¼	cup Dijon mustard
2	tablespoons whole-grain mustard
2	tablespoons honey
2	garlic cloves, minced
2	tablespoons chopped fresh rosemary leaves
1	(3½-pound) center-cut, boneless pork loin roast
12	slices (about 1 pound) bacon

salad

3	tablespoons fresh lemon juice (from 1 lemon)
3	tablespoons olive oil
	Salt and freshly ground black pepper
5	cups (5 ounces) baby arugula

special equipment

Kitchen twine

For the roast: Place an oven rack in the lower third of the oven and preheat the oven to 350°F.

In a small bowl, mix together the Dijon mustard, whole-grain mustard, honey, garlic, and rosemary until smooth. Spread the mustard mixture evenly over the pork. Starting at one end, wrap a piece of bacon around the pork. Wrap another slice of bacon around the pork, making sure to slightly overlap the first piece. Continue with the remaining bacon until the pork is fully wrapped in bacon. Using 6 to 8 pieces of kitchen twine, tied at regular intervals around the roast, secure the bacon in place.

Place the pork in a 9 x 13-inch baking pan and roast for 1 hour. Cover the pan loosely with foil and roast for another 10 to 20 minutes, until a meat thermometer inserted into the thickest part of the pork registers 160°F. Remove from the oven. Cover the pan with foil again and allow the pork roast to rest for 20 minutes. Remove the kitchen twine and slice the meat into ¼-inch-thick slices.

For the salad: While the pork is resting, in a small bowl, whisk together the lemon juice and oil until smooth. Season the dressing with salt and pepper.

Arrange the arugula on a large platter and drizzle with the dressing. Lay the pork slices on top and serve.

roasted branzino with lemons

4 SERVINGS

Cooking a fish whole is the best way to ensure it will stay moist and flavorful, and the process is a lot less intimidating than it looks. Branzino is a small Mediterranean sea bass with a mild flavor and delicate texture, enhanced here with a bright, fresh stuffing of fennel and lemon. Todd says he always feels like he's on a diet when he eats fish, so I cook it with some pancetta to hearty up the dish a bit. Do watch out for small bones when you serve the branzino.

2	teaspoons olive oil
8	ounces pancetta, cut into ¼-inch dice
	Vegetable oil cooking spray
2	(1½-pound) whole branzino, striped bass, or red snapper, scaled and gutted, head removed
	Salt and freshly ground black pepper
2	lemons, zest grated, thinly sliced
1	medium fennel bulb, fronds coarsely chopped (about ¼ cup) and bulb trimmed and thinly sliced
2	tablespoons chopped fresh thyme leaves
½	cup dry white wine

Place an oven rack in the lower third of the oven. Preheat the oven to 400°F.

In a small skillet, heat the oil over medium-high heat. Add the pancetta and cook, stirring occasionally, until brown and crispy, about 8 to 10 minutes. Drain on paper towels. Set aside.

Lay a piece of heavy-duty foil on a baking sheet. Spray the foil with vegetable oil cooking spray. Lay the fish in the center of the foil and cut two 2-inch diagonal slits on each side of each fish, taking care not to cut through the bone. Season the cavities with salt and pepper. In a small bowl, mix together half of the lemon zest, the fennel fronds, and thyme. Divide the mixture in half and place in the cavities. Stuff the fish with the lemon and fennel slices, reserving 4 lemon slices to place on top. Scatter any remaining fennel and the cooked pancetta around the fish. Pour the wine over the fish and arrange

recipe continues

2 lemon slices on top of each. Lay another piece of foil on top and crimp the edges of both pieces of foil together to form a packet.

Roast the fish for 30 to 35 minutes, until the flesh is flaky and cooked through. Let rest for 5 minutes. Carefully remove the top piece of foil. Transfer the fish to a cutting board. Remove the fennel and lemon slices and arrange on a platter. Pull back the skin from the fish. Using a sharp knife, separate the two top fillets from the backbone. Using a metal spatula, transfer the fillets to the platter. Lift the fish backbone from the bottom fillets (the backbone should come off easily) and discard. Using the spatula, transfer the two remaining fillets to the platter. Sprinkle with the remaining lemon zest before serving.

red snapper
with fava bean purée

4 SERVINGS

I love the look, flavor, and textures of this delicate and pretty dish. It's a perfect way to spotlight the flavors of spring, when fava beans are in season. Other times of the year you can substitute frozen lima beans for the favas; either way the purée is bright from the mint and satisfies your starch cravings. Just be careful not to overcook the beans, as they can turn an unattractive gray. Red snapper, with its pinkish hue, is a quite flavorful white fish that works perfectly with the fava beans. Finish it off with a drizzle of really good-quality extra-virgin olive oil.

4	cups (1 quart) low-sodium chicken broth
3	pounds fresh fava beans, shelled, or 1½ pounds frozen lima beans, thawed
3	tablespoons chopped fresh mint leaves
	Salt and freshly ground black pepper
3	tablespoons olive oil
4	(6-ounce) center-cut red snapper fillets

In a medium saucepan, bring the broth to a boil over medium-high heat. Add the beans. Reduce the heat to low and simmer until the beans are tender, 5 to 8 minutes. Drain the beans and reserve 1 cup of the broth. If using fava beans, when the beans are cool enough to handle, pop them out of their outer pods, discarding the pods. Combine the fava or lima beans and reserved broth in a blender or food processor. Add the mint and blend until smooth. Season with salt and pepper.

In a large skillet, heat the olive oil over medium-high heat. Season the fish with salt and pepper on both sides. Cook for 3 to 4 minutes on each side, until brown and the center is just opaque.

Divide the fava bean purée among 4 serving plates. Place a fillet of red snapper on top of the purée. Serve immediately.

grilled salmon with citrus salsa verde

4 SERVINGS

This is my favorite way to eat fish, with a very clean, fresh, and simple preparation. Agave is a natural sweetener from the blue agave plant in South America, and brushed on the salmon it creates a nice caramelized crust. Topped with salsa verde made of citrus zests and herbs, this dish is super-light and perfect on a hot summer day. Jade loves the grilled salmon, too!

salsa

2	large oranges
1	teaspoon grated lemon zest
3	tablespoons fresh lemon juice (from 1 lemon)
¼	cup olive oil
½	cup chopped fresh flat-leaf parsley leaves
2	scallions, finely sliced
3	tablespoons chopped fresh mint leaves
2	tablespoons capers, rinsed, drained, and coarsely chopped
1	teaspoon crushed red pepper flakes
	Salt and freshly ground black pepper

salmon

	Vegetable or canola oil, for the grill
4	(4- to 5-ounce) skinless center-cut salmon fillets, each about 3 inches square
2	tablespoons amber agave nectar or pure maple syrup
	Salt and freshly ground black pepper

For the salsa: Grate 2 tablespoons zest from the oranges and put it in a medium bowl. Peel and trim the ends from each orange with a sharp knife. Using a paring knife, cut along the membrane on both sides of each segment. Free the segments and place on a cutting board. Coarsely chop the segments and scoop them into the bowl with the orange zest. Add the lemon zest, lemon juice, olive oil, parsley, scallions, mint, capers, and red pepper flakes. Toss lightly and season with salt and pepper. Set aside.

For the salmon: Place a grill pan over medium-high heat or preheat a gas or charcoal grill. Brush the grilling rack with vegetable oil to keep the salmon from sticking.

Brush the salmon on both sides with the agave nectar and season with salt and pepper. Grill for 3 to 4 minutes on each side, until the fish flakes easily and is cooked to medium. Transfer the salmon to a platter and allow to rest for 5 minutes.

Spoon the salsa verde on top of the salmon, or serve it on the side as an accompaniment.

roasted halibut with pea and mint salad

SERVES 4

If you're in the mood for a light but filling dish, look no further. Halibut is low in fat but delicate, sweet, and flaky, and it embraces the flavors of most anything you pair it with. I like to marinate and then roast halibut before serving it on top of a colorful, warm spring salad of peas and mint. This is my kind of food.

fish

- ¼ cup fresh lemon juice (from 1 to 2 lemons)
- ¼ cup olive oil
- 2 garlic cloves, minced
- ½ teaspoon salt
- ¼ teaspoon freshly ground black pepper
- 4 (6-ounce) skinless center-cut halibut fillets
  Vegetable oil cooking spray

salad

- 5 tablespoons olive oil
- 2 large or 4 small shallots, thinly sliced
- 1 large red bell pepper, cored, seeded, and sliced into ¼-inch-thick slices
  Salt and freshly ground black pepper
- 1½ cups frozen petite peas, thawed
- 1 packed cup plus 2 tablespoons chopped fresh mint leaves
- 1 tablespoon grated lemon zest (from 1 lemon)
- 1 tablespoon chopped fresh thyme leaves

For the fish: In a small bowl, whisk together the lemon juice, olive oil, garlic, salt, and pepper until smooth. Pour the mixture into a resealable plastic bag. Add the halibut and coat with the lemon mixture. Refrigerate for 30 minutes.

Place an oven rack in the center of the oven and preheat the oven to 400° F. Spray a small rimmed baking sheet or glass baking dish with vegetable oil cooking spray.

Remove the halibut from the marinade and arrange on the prepared baking sheet. Roast for 15 to 18 minutes, until the fish flakes easily and is cooked through.

For the salad: Heat 3 tablespoons of the olive oil in a medium skillet over medium-high heat. Add the shallots and bell pepper. Season with salt and pepper. Cook, stirring frequently, until the shallots are soft and translucent, about 6 minutes. Remove the pan from the heat. Add the peas, 1 cup chopped mint, the lemon zest and thyme. Drizzle with the remaining 2 tablespoons of olive oil and stir to combine. Season with salt and pepper.

Spoon the salad onto 4 plates and top each with a halibut fillet. Garnish with the remaining 2 tablespoons chopped mint and serve.

vegetables
& salads

Pecorino and Bean Salad ✤

Grilled Asparagus and Melon Salad

Skewered Greek Salad

Fresh Mushroom and Parsley Salad ✤

Bibb, Basil, and Mint Salad with Parmesan Butter Crostini

Arugula Salad with Roasted Fruit and Panettone Croutons

Roasted Tomatoes with Garlic, Gorgonzola, and Herbs ✤

Vegetable Fritto Misto with Lemon Mayonnaise ✤

Grilled and Stuffed Portobello Mushrooms with Gorgonzola ✤

Olive and Sun-Dried Tomato Vegetables

Vegetable Parmesan

Italian Lentil Salad ✤

Sweet and Savory Bread Pudding

Cauliflower and Pancetta Gratinata ✤

In my humble opinion, vegetables are what give a meal its plate appeal, and I would never consider a meal complete without some green—or orange or yellow or red. In fact I'd sooner skip the meat than my veggies.

When we moved to California one of the strangest things to my brother, sister, and me was the American way with vegetables. Without question Italians like their veggies cooked to the point Americans might consider overcooked, especially here in California, where we like them a little on the al dente side. After much consideration, though, I have to say each approach has something to recommend it. Long cooking, specifically low-slow roasting and stewing, concentrates and intensifies the flavor of many vegetables, especially if they are not at the height of seasonal freshness. A great example of this is the Roasted Tomatoes with Garlic, Gorgonzola, and Herbs (page 155), which is sumptuous even made with supermarket plum tomatoes. On the other hand, quick cooking at high temperature preserves the texture and color of vegetables. My Vegetable Fritto Misto with Lemon Mayonnaise (page 156), which has the unexpected twist of fried garbanzo beans and lemon slices along with lots of gorgeous fried vegetables, is a perfect illustration of how vibrant flash-cooked veggies can be.

Salads are popular both here and in Italy—I grew up eating bitter greens like arugula and radicchio—but in California salad-making has been elevated to an art, and greens are just the beginning of what you might find in a salad bowl. The simple arugula salad of my childhood has morphed into Arugula Salad with Roasted Fruit and Panettone Croutons (page 152), and even a Greek salad gets a new spin when it's assembled onto skewers and served as finger food (see page 146). So, go old world or new wave—just be sure to eat your veggies!

pecorino and bean salad

4 TO 6 SERVINGS

A classic example of the type of salads you'll find in Italy, this is easy to throw together and more impressive than the usual mixed green salad. Depending on the region, the type of cheese may differ. I love to nibble on chunks of Pecorino as I make it.

12	ounces green beans, trimmed and cut into 1-inch pieces (about 2 cups)
3	tablespoons olive oil
3	garlic cloves, minced
2	teaspoons finely chopped fresh rosemary leaves
1	(15-ounce) can cannellini beans, rinsed and drained
5	ounces Pecorino Romano cheese, cut into ¼-inch chunks (1 cup)
¼	cup chopped fresh flat-leaf parsley leaves
¼	teaspoon salt
¼	teaspoon finely ground black pepper

Bring a medium saucepan of salted water to a boil over high heat. Add the green beans and cook for 3 minutes, or until vibrant green but still crisp. Drain and place in a bowl of ice water for 1 minute. Drain and set aside.

In a small nonstick skillet, heat the oil over medium-low heat. Add the garlic and cook until fragrant, but not brown, about 30 seconds. Remove the pan from the heat. Stir in the rosemary and let cool slightly.

Combine the green beans, cannellini beans, Pecorino cheese, parsley, salt, and pepper in a serving bowl. Add the garlic-rosemary oil and toss well, until all the ingredients are coated.

grilled asparagus and melon salad

4 TO 6 SERVINGS

This salad is a new twist on the classic combo of melon and prosciutto. Grilled asparagus keeps a slight crunch and also has a smoky char to it that pairs with the creaminess and subtle flavor of mozzarella and the fruitiness of melon. To top it off: crumbled prosciutto. I've always loved the salty tang of prosciutto, but since I started baking thin slices of it to make brittle, crispy chips, my love has become a full-blown obsession; they just seem to make everything taste better.

2	ounces thinly sliced prosciutto
2	tablespoons pine nuts
1	pound asparagus, trimmed
2	tablespoons plus 2 teaspoons olive oil
	Salt and freshly ground black pepper
2	tablespoons fresh lemon juice (from 1 lemon)
1/4	small melon (about 12 ounces), peeled, seeded, and cut into 3/4-inch cubes
4	ounces fresh mozzarella or burrata cheese, cut into 3/4-inch cubes

Place an oven rack in the center of the oven and preheat the oven to 350°F.

Line a rimmed baking sheet with parchment paper. Place the prosciutto in a single layer on the prepared baking sheet. Bake for 12 to 14 minutes, until crispy. Drain the prosciutto on paper towels and set aside to cool. Chop the prosciutto into 1/4-inch pieces.

Meanwhile, heat a small, heavy skillet over medium-low heat. Add the pine nuts to the hot skillet and stir them until they become fragrant and golden brown, about 5 minutes. Transfer to a plate to cool.

Place a grill pan over medium-high heat or preheat a gas or charcoal grill.

In a medium bowl, toss together the asparagus and 2 teaspoons of the olive oil. Season with salt and pepper. Grill for 2 to 3 minutes on each side until crisp-tender.

In a medium bowl, combine the lemon juice and remaining 2 tablespoons olive oil. Whisk until combined. Season with salt and pepper. Add the melon and mozzarella cheese. Toss to coat.

Arrange the asparagus on a platter. Spoon the melon and mozzarella cheese on top of the asparagus. Drizzle any remaining dressing from the bowl over the top. Sprinkle with the prosciutto and pine nuts and serve.

skewered greek salad

4 TO 6 SERVINGS

It's amazing how simple wooden skewers can transform a dinner standby into cocktail party fare! These look beautiful as part of a buffet spread but work equally well as a passed hors d'oeuvre since there's no need for a plate. Best of all, they can be made well ahead of time; just wait to add the vinaigrette until right before serving. Elegant and simple.

skewers

24	grape or small cherry tomatoes
3	ounces firm feta cheese (see Cook's Note), cut into 12 (1/2-inch) cubes
12	pitted kalamata olives
1/2	small red or sweet onion, cut into 12 (1/2-inch) pieces

vinaigrette

2	teaspoons fresh lemon juice
2	teaspoons red wine vinegar
4	teaspoons chopped fresh oregano leaves
2	tablespoons olive oil
	Salt and freshly ground black pepper

special equipment

12	(6-inch) bamboo or wood skewers

For the skewers: Thread the skewers starting with a tomato, then a cube of feta cheese, an olive, a piece of onion, and finally another tomato. Repeat with the remaining ingredients and skewers.

For the vinaigrette: In a small bowl, mix together the lemon juice, red wine vinegar, and half of the oregano. Whisk in the olive oil until the mixture thickens. Season with salt and pepper.

Arrange the skewers on a serving platter. Spoon the vinaigrette over the skewers and sprinkle with the remaining oregano.

COOK'S NOTE: Buy feta packed in water; it is moist and easier to skewer, and it won't crumble.

fresh mushroom and parsley salad

4 SERVINGS

There are only so many plain green salads anyone can eat. I remember having a mushroom salad with plenty of parsley in it in Rome and the herby, earthy combination was just the right balance of light and substantial. It makes an unusual and very tasty counterpoint to any kind of roasted meat.

¼	cup olive oil
¼	cup fresh lemon juice (from 1 to 2 lemons)
	Salt and freshly ground black pepper
1	pound large button mushrooms, trimmed, cleaned, and thinly sliced
⅓	cup chopped fresh flat-leaf parsley leaves
1	(2-ounce) piece of Parmesan cheese

In a medium salad bowl, whisk together the oil and lemon juice until smooth. Season with salt and pepper. Add the mushrooms and parsley and toss to coat.

Using a vegetable peeler, shave the Parmesan cheese on top and serve.

bibb, basil, and mint salad with parmesan butter crostini

4 TO 6 SERVINGS

You always need a simple, elegant green salad in your repertoire. What I love are the buttery and cheesy crostini, so you get your healthy, leafy vegetable with a little indulgence.

crostini

½	baguette loaf, cut into ½-inch-thick slices
¼	cup (½ stick) unsalted butter, at room temperature
⅓	cup freshly grated Parmesan cheese

salad

3	tablespoons fresh lemon juice (from 1 lemon)
3	tablespoons olive oil
	Salt and freshly ground black pepper
1	head Bibb or butter lettuce, leaves torn
1	medium fennel bulb, trimmed and thinly sliced
⅓	packed cup fresh basil leaves, chopped
⅓	packed cup fresh mint leaves, chopped

For the crostini: Place an oven rack in the lower third of the oven and preheat the oven to 375°F.

Arrange the bread slices in a single layer on a rimmed baking sheet. Bake for 10 to 12 minutes, until golden.

Meanwhile, in a small bowl, using a fork, mix the butter and cheese together until smooth.

For the salad: In a salad bowl, whisk together the lemon juice and oil until smooth. Season with salt and pepper. Add the lettuce, fennel, basil, and mint and toss well.

Spread the Parmesan butter on the crostini and serve alongside the salad.

olive oil

People ask me all the time how to choose a good olive oil. There are some general rules to consider, but in the end the choice is a subjective one. I am, of course, partial to Italian varieties, but there are excellent Spanish, Greek, Californian, even Australian olive oils on the market. To further complicate things, olives are often imported from one area to be pressed and bottled in another. The only sure way to find your favorite is to taste a few to discover which you like best.

There are thousands of varieties of olives, and each has its own unique qualities, flavors, and characteristics. Since olive oils can vary in hue—from deep, grassy green to bright yellow—color is not an accurate indicator of flavor. However, all good olive oils, share three qualities: fruitiness, bitterness, and pungency. Finding an oil with a balance of these three traits that pleases your palate is the key. I like those with mainly fruity and peppery characteristics (the peppery pungency reminds me of arugula), but other people prefer a bitter edge to their oil. Again, it's all about personal preference.

If you're going to spend the money, though, make sure the oil you're buying is certified virgin or extra-virgin, which means it was made from the olives' first pressing and contains no chemicals, solvents, or additives (the level of acidity in the oil determines whether it is virgin or "extra"-virgin). Oils labeled simply "olive oil" contain a blend of virgin oil and more acidic oils that have been refined to minimize their acidity and make them more palatable.

When selecting an extra-virgin oil, look for one that is labeled by date, and don't buy any that is more than a year old. The bottle should be dark, heavy glass to protect the oil from light, heat, and humidity—all of which can penetrate a clear glass or plastic container and cause a perfectly good oil to go bad. If you taste hints of dirt, mold, or rancidness, or if your olive oil has gone flat, then it's time to throw the oil away.

I also look for the word *filtered* on olive oil labels. This means that during processing, any particles of pit, flesh, leaf, or other materials have been strained out of the final product. The result is a cleaner olive oil.

As for when to use regular olive oil instead of extra-virgin? I use regular to sauté and fry foods, since it is relatively inexpensive and has a higher smoke point (so it can be heated to a higher temperature without burning). I save the more expensive extra-virgin olive oil for dressing raw foods and salads and for drizzling sparingly onto a finished dish almost like a seasoning—it enhances every bite.

arugula salad with roasted fruit and panettone croutons

6 SERVINGS

At Christmastime in Italy every visitor seems to show up with a panettone for his host, meaning most homes end up with lots of extra panettone. I've become pretty creative when it comes to finding new uses for this delicious, fruit-laden yeast bread. Bread pudding is one obvious possibility, but I once cut some up for croutons and thought they were sensational. Combined with candy-sweet roasted fruits and peppery arugula, they make a very sophisticated dish to serve with poached eggs for brunch or alongside grilled chicken or chops.

3	cups 1-inch cubed panettone (about 6 ounces)
1	cup fresh or thawed frozen cranberries
1	cup red seedless grapes
2	Bartlett pears, cut into eighths and cored
2	plums, cut into eighths and pitted
2	tablespoons unsalted butter, melted
1/4	cup plus 2 tablespoons lemon juice (from 2 lemons)
1	tablespoon sugar
1/4	cup honey, preferably orange blossom
1/4	cup canola oil
2	tablespoons heavy cream
	Grated zest of 1/2 lemon
	Salt and freshly ground black pepper
6	cups (6 ounces) arugula

Preheat the oven to 300°F.

Spread out the panettone cubes on a parchment paper–lined rimmed baking sheet. Bake until dark golden brown and crispy on the outside, 45 to 50 minutes. Remove from the oven and set aside. The croutons will continue to crisp up as they cool.

Increase the oven temperature to 425°F.

Place the fruit in a large mixing bowl and drizzle with the butter, 2 table-spoons of the lemon juice, and the sugar. Toss to coat and spread the fruit out in a single layer on a parchment paper–lined rimmed baking sheet. Bake until the pears are tender and the fruit is beginning to brown on the edges, 25 to 30 minutes. Remove from the oven and set aside.

Meanwhile, combine the honey, the remaining ¼ cup lemon juice, the canola oil, cream, lemon zest, 1 teaspoon salt, and ¼ teaspoon pepper in a blender. Run the machine until the ingredients are well blended. Set aside.

To assemble the salad, place the arugula, roasted fruit, and panettone croutons in a large bowl. Add the salad dressing, ½ teaspoon salt, and ¼ teaspoon pepper. Toss to coat and serve immediately.

roasted tomatoes with garlic, gorgonzola, and herbs

6 TO 8 SERVINGS

Tomatoes are a staple ingredient in Italian cooking, and this dish is inspired by the beautiful image of vast fields of sweet vine-ripened tomatoes that are a common sight in southern Italy. The bright, concentrated flavors of the tomatoes in this dish make them a great simple accompaniment to grilled fish or meats. Actually, they are so delicious you'll want to serve them on their own as an antipasto; just pop them right into your mouth. Each tomato holds its shape as it cooks and becomes sweet and tender, with a golden crust and gooey cheese in the center. My mouth waters just thinking about it!

12	plum tomatoes, sliced in half lengthwise
4	tablespoons olive oil
2	garlic cloves, minced
1/2	teaspoon salt
1/2	teaspoon freshly ground black pepper
3/4	cup plain dried bread crumbs
3/4	cup (3 ounces) finely crumbled Gorgonzola cheese
2	tablespoons chopped fresh flat-leaf parsley leaves

Preheat the oven to 375°F.

Using a teaspoon or grapefruit spoon, remove the seeds from the tomatoes. Place the tomato halves, cut side down, on paper towels to drain, about 5 minutes.

In a large bowl, mix together 2 tablespoons of the olive oil, the garlic, salt, and pepper. Using clean hands, gently toss the drained tomato halves in the oil mixture until coated. Marinate the tomatoes for 10 minutes.

In a small bowl, mix together the bread crumbs and Gorgonzola cheese.

Place the marinated tomato halves, cut side up, on a rimmed baking sheet limed with parchment paper. Fill each tomato half with the bread crumb filling. Drizzle with the remaining olive oil. Bake for 20 to 25 minutes, until the tomatoes are slightly softened and their undersides are brown.

Arrange the cooked tomatoes on a serving platter and sprinkle with parsley.

vegetable fritto misto with lemon mayonnaise

4 TO 6 SERVINGS

Fritto misto means mixed fry, and in Italy, where it is a great way to use up odds and ends from the kitchen, it might contain meat, cheese, fish—anything that can be breaded and fried (and what can't, really?). My favorite part of any fritto misto is always the veggies, and this version is nothing but. It has the added surprise of fried garbanzos, which get crunchy on the outside and creamy within, and lemon slices, which are crispy and delicious.

	Vegetable oil, for frying
2	large eggs, lightly beaten
1½	cups all-purpose flour
2	teaspoons fine salt
1	teaspoon freshly ground black pepper
1	small cauliflower, cut into 1-inch florets
4	ounces green beans, halved
1	fennel bulb, trimmed and sliced ¼ inch thick
1	cup canned garbanzo beans, drained and rinsed
1	lemon, sliced ¼ inch thick
1	cup mayonnaise
2	tablespoons fresh lemon juice (from 1 lemon)

In a large, heavy-bottomed saucepan, pour enough oil to fill the pan a third of the way. Heat over medium heat until a deep frying thermometer inserted in the oil reaches 375°F. (If you don't have a thermometer, toss in a cube of bread; it will brown in about 3 minutes and, when it does, the oil is ready.)

While the oil heats, in a medium bowl, mix together the eggs and 2 tablespoons water. In another medium bowl, mix together the flour, salt, and pepper. Dip the cauliflower in the egg mixture, allowing any extra egg mixture to drip off. Dredge the cauliflower in the flour mixture. Fry the cauliflower for 1 to 3 minutes, until lightly browned. Drain on paper towels. Repeat the battering and frying with the green beans, fennel, garbanzos beans, and finally the lemon slices.

In a small bowl, whisk together the mayonnaise and lemon juice until smooth. Arrange the fritto misto on a platter and serve with the lemon mayonnaise.

grilled and stuffed portobello mushrooms with gorgonzola

6 SERVINGS

Portobello mushrooms are one of the most versatile, hearty, and prized ingredients in Italian cooking. When I see large, meaty portobellos at the grocery store, I immediately think of all the ways my mother prepared them, and one of my favorites was grilled and stuffed with sausage, Gorgonzola, and fresh herbs. Serve the mushrooms as a side dish or as a meal in itself. Either way, you'll be surprised at how quickly they disappear.

1/4   cup plus 2 tablespoons olive oil

12   ounces turkey sausage, casings removed

2   garlic cloves, minced

1/2   cup (4 ounces) mascarpone cheese, at room temperature

2   tablespoons fresh thyme leaves

2   tablespoons fresh oregano leaves

3/4   cup plain dried bread crumbs

1   cup (4 ounces) crumbled Gorgonzola cheese

     Salt and freshly ground black pepper

6   large portobello mushrooms, stems removed

In a large skillet, heat 2 tablespoons of the oil over medium-high heat. Add the turkey sausage and cook, stirring frequently, until cooked through, about 5 minutes. Add the garlic and cook for 1 minute. Remove the pan from the heat. Stir in the mascarpone cheese, thyme, oregano, bread crumbs, ½ cup of the Gorgonzola cheese, ½ teaspoon salt, and ½ teaspoon pepper.

Place a grill pan over medium-high heat or preheat a gas or charcoal grill.

Brush the mushrooms on both sides with the remaining ¼ cup oil and season with salt and pepper. Grill them, stem side down, for 3 minutes. Turn them over and grill the other sides for 2 minutes, or until tender.

Fill the mushrooms with the sausage mixture and top with the remaining ½ cup Gorgonzola cheese. Grill them, stuffing side up, until the stuffing is warmed through, 5 to 7 minutes.

olive and sun-dried tomato vegetables

2 SERVINGS

Much as I love vegetables, sometimes even I get a bit bored of the same old same old, and I'm always looking for easy ways to jazz up plain sautéed vegetables. I've found that adding something sweet and salty nearly always does the trick, and this colorful mix is a case in point. I always make extras so I can snack on leftovers the next day, adding some crusty bread for sopping up the flavorful vegetable juices.

1/3	cup plus 3 tablespoons olive oil
5	oil-packed sun-dried tomatoes, drained and finely chopped
2	tablespoons halved pitted small black olives, such as kalamata
2	tablespoons halved pitted green olives
1/4	teaspoon dried thyme
	Salt and freshly ground black pepper
3	shallots, thinly sliced
1	zucchini, ends trimmed, cut into 1/2-inch rounds
1	yellow summer squash, ends trimmed, cut into 1/2-inch rounds
1	small red bell pepper, cored, seeded, and cut into 1/4-inch strips

In a medium bowl, whisk together the 1/3 cup olive oil, the sun-dried tomatoes, black and green olives, and thyme. Season with salt and pepper.

In a medium skillet, heat the remaining 3 tablespoons oil over medium-high heat. Add the shallots and cook until translucent and tender, 2 to 3 minutes. Add the zucchini, yellow squash, bell pepper, and 1/2 teaspoon salt. Cook, stirring frequently, for 6 to 8 minutes, until the vegetables are tender.

Add the warm vegetables to the olive and sun-dried tomato mixture and toss until coated. Transfer to a serving bowl and serve immediately.

vegetable parmesan

4 TO 6 SERVINGS

Of all the recipes I've done for *Giada at Home* on TV, this one has been the biggest hit with both viewers and my crew. I've always said that if you want to get kids (and picky adults) to eat something, bake it with marinara and cheese and they'll be demanding seconds. You'll be happy because they're eating lots of healthy veggies, they'll be happy because it tastes awesome, and as an added bonus, your kitchen will smell fantastic, too. Use any vegetable that you love or have on hand in this dish; it's very versatile.

	Unsalted butter, for the pan
1	medium eggplant, cut into ¼- to ½-inch-thick slices
2	medium fennel bulbs, trimmed and sliced ¼ inch thick
1	red bell pepper, cored, seeded, and cut into thirds
1	yellow bell pepper, cored, seeded, and cut into thirds
1	orange bell pepper, cored, seeded, and cut into thirds
¼	cup olive oil, plus more for drizzling
	Salt and freshly ground black pepper
1	(26-ounce) jar marinara sauce (3⅓ cups)
3	cups (12 ounces) shredded mozzarella cheese
1	cup freshly grated Parmesan cheese
1	cup plain dried bread crumbs

Place a grill pan over medium-high heat or preheat a gas or charcoal grill. Place an oven rack in the center of the oven and preheat the oven to 375°F. Butter a 13 x 9-inch glass baking dish.

Toss the eggplant, fennel, and bell peppers with the ¼ cup olive oil. Season with salt and pepper. Grill the vegetables for 3 to 4 minutes on each side, or until softened.

Spoon ¾ cup of the marinara sauce over the bottom of the prepared baking dish. Arrange the eggplant slices on top. Sprinkle with 1 cup of the mozzarella cheese and ⅓ cup of the Parmesan cheese. Arrange the peppers in a single layer on top. Spoon ¾ cup of the marinara sauce over the peppers. Sprinkle with 1 cup of the mozzarella cheese and ⅓ cup of the Parmesan cheese. Layer the fennel on top and cover with the remaining sauce. Sprinkle the remaining mozzarella and Parmesan cheeses on top. Sprinkle the bread crumbs over the cheese and drizzle with olive oil.

Bake for 30 to 35 minutes, until the top is golden and forms a crust. Let cool for 10 minutes before serving.

COOK'S NOTE: The vegetables can also be baked in a 375ºF oven for 15 to 20 minutes, or until softened.

italian lentil salad

Italians love lentils and cook them in lots of creative ways, including the traditional lentil and sausage dish that is served on New Year's Day. Lentils are also very often used as the basis of a main-course salad like this one, which is a little more refined than most thanks to the sweet, juicy grapes and chopped hazelnuts. Like lentil soup, this salad develops more flavor the longer it sits, and it makes a wonderful bed for flavorful fish such as salmon. Certainly you can eat this right away, or make it ahead of time, refrigerate overnight, and serve at room temperature the next day.

1	pound green lentils
2	scallions, white part only, chopped
1	cup halved seedless green grapes
1	cup halved seedless red grapes
1	cucumber, peeled, seeded, and diced
1	red bell pepper, cored, seeded, and diced
1/2	cup coarsely chopped skinned and toasted hazelnuts
2	teaspoons grated lemon zest (from 1 to 2 lemons)
1/3	cup fresh lemon juice (from 2 lemons)
1/3	cup olive oil
1/2	teaspoon salt
1/4	teaspoon freshly ground black pepper

Bring a large pot of salted water to a boil over high heat. Add the lentils and cook until tender, stirring occasionally, 18 to 20 minutes. Drain and let cool for 5 minutes.

Combine the lentils, scallions, red and green grapes, cucumber, bell pepper, hazelnuts, and lemon zest in a large salad bowl.

Pour the lemon juice into a small bowl. Slowly add the oil, whisking constantly, until combined. Season the dressing with salt and pepper.

Pour the dressing over the salad and toss well.

sweet and savory bread pudding

6 TO 8 SERVINGS

Why should stuffing be only a once- or twice-a-year treat? A savory bread pudding has all the comfort food flavors of stuffing with no need for the bird. This one is especially delicious, packed with homey winter vegetables and a hint of sweetness and spice. Serve it at your holiday feast or with any meal you want to make a touch more festive.

2	tablespoons olive oil or unsalted butter, plus more for the pan
1	pound butternut squash, peeled and cut into 3/4-inch pieces
4	parsnips, peeled and cut into 3/4-inch pieces
	Salt and freshly ground black pepper
1	(1-pound) loaf of brioche, challah, or sourdough bread, cut or torn into 1-inch pieces
3	cups heavy cream
8	large eggs, beaten
1/2	cup brandy
1/4	cup vegetable oil
3	tablespoons light brown sugar
1 1/2	tablespoons ground cinnamon
1	tablespoon fresh thyme leaves, chopped

Place an oven rack in the center of the oven and preheat the oven to 375°F. Grease a 9 x 13-inch glass baking dish. Set aside.

In a large skillet, heat the olive oil over medium-high heat. Add the butternut squash and parsnips. Season with salt and pepper. Cook, stirring occasionally, for 8 minutes, or until slightly softened. Set aside to cool.

Put the bread in a large bowl. In another large bowl, combine the heavy cream, eggs, and brandy. Whisk in 2 teaspoons salt, 1 teaspoon pepper, the vegetable oil, brown sugar, cinnamon, and thyme until smooth. Pour the cream mixture over the bread. Add the cooled vegetables and toss until the bread and vegetables are coated. Spoon the mixture into the prepared baking dish.

Bake for 40 to 45 minutes, until the bread pudding is puffed and golden (cover the pan with foil if the top becomes too brown during baking).

cauliflower and pancetta gratinata

4 TO 6 SERVINGS

This is a cross between a traditional gratin and a savory bread pudding, and trust me, cauliflower has never tasted so good. Pancetta, cheese, cream sauce—need I say more?

8	ounces thinly sliced pancetta
4	tablespoons (1/2 stick) unsalted butter, cut into 1/2-inch pieces, plus more for the baking dish
1	pound cauliflower, trimmed and cut into florets
2	cups plain dried bread crumbs
3/4	cup heavy cream
1	teaspoon all-purpose flour
1/4	cup capers, rinsed and drained
1	cup (4 ounces) grated Gruyère cheese
	Salt and freshly ground black pepper
	Olive oil, for drizzling

Place an oven rack in the center of the oven and preheat the oven to 400°F.

Arrange the pancetta slices in a single layer on two rimmed baking sheets. Bake until crisp, 10 to 12 minutes. Set aside to cool. Crumble the pancetta.

Lower the oven temperature to 350°F. Butter an 8 x 8-inch baking dish. Set aside.

Bring a medium saucepan of salted water to a boil over high heat. Add the cauliflower and cook for 2 minutes. Drain well in a colander for about 5 minutes.

In a large nonstick skillet, heat the butter over medium heat. Add the bread crumbs and cook, stirring constantly, until all the butter has been absorbed and the bread crumbs are toasted, 1 to 2 minutes.

In a medium bowl, whisk together the cream and flour. Add the cauliflower, capers, pancetta, and 1/2 cup of the Gruyère cheese. Season with salt and pepper. Pour the cauliflower mixture into the prepared baking dish. Sprinkle with the bread crumbs and the remaining 1/2 cup cheese. Drizzle with olive oil.

Bake the gratinata for 35 to 40 minutes, until the cheese has melted and the top is golden brown.

desserts

Poached Pears in Honey, Ginger, and Cinnamon Syrup ❈

Ricotta with Vanilla-Sugar Croutons and Berry Syrup

Espresso Chip Meringues

Apricot and Nut Cookies with Amaretto Icing ❈

Espresso Caramel Bars

Cranberry Cornmeal Cake ❈

White Chocolate–Dipped Almond and Lemon Biscotti ❈

Raspberry Pound Cake with Vin Santo Cream

Chocolate Rice Pudding ❈

Lemon Hazelnut Tiramisù

Limoncello Granita ❈

Chocolate Honey Almond Tart

Pomegranate and Mint Sorbet

There is more to Italian desserts than gelato and biscotti. Generally, the desserts vary by region, with those served in the north tending to be more creamy and heavy, while those found in southern Italy are generally fruit-based and a little lighter. Many of them aren't all that sweet; Cranberry Cornmeal Cake (page 183) could easily be served as an afternoon pick-me-up and Poached Pears in Honey, Ginger, and Cinnamon Syrup (page 173) as a nice, simple finale for a holiday meal. But though the Italian repertoire of desserts isn't huge, there are a few classics, such as Limoncello Granita (page 193) and Apricot and Nut Cookies with Amaretto Icing (page 178), that are deservedly well-loved, and I hope you'll try them.

Because I love dessert so much, however, I couldn't resist tinkering with some of these old standbys, jazzing them up with the addition of unexpected flavors. If I do say so myself, I think many of these are even better than the originals. Adding lots of fresh lemon to tiramisù makes it light as a feather and twice as refreshing, and combining pomegranate and mint in a sorbet—not so different from an Italian granita—makes the perfect, palate-cleansing finish to a heavy meal. Italians often use honey in their baked goods, and I do, too. When it's added to chocolate in my Chocolate Honey Almond Tart (page 194), it satisfies the cravings of any chocoholic—including me. It's sweet and always leaves a smile on my face, which as far as I'm concerned is really the whole point of any good dessert, isn't it?

poached pears in honey, ginger, and cinnamon syrup

6 SERVINGS

Moscato is not well known in this country, but this sweet, fizzy wine is very often served at the end of Italian meals along with dessert or just some cheese and fruit. Here I use it to poach beautiful whole pears; the cinnamon poaching liquid is then reduced to a syrup. It's the perfect ending to a Thanksgiving dinner because it's not too sweet or too heavy, and it's absolutely gorgeous on the plate—not to mention how it fills the whole house with holiday fragrance. Serve flutes of chilled Moscato alongside for a very elegant finish to a fancy meal.

1½   cups sugar

1   (750 ml) bottle Moscato wine or other sweet dessert wine

2   cinnamon sticks

2   tablespoons honey

1   (¾-inch) piece of fresh ginger, peeled and finely chopped

1   vanilla bean, split lengthwise

6   small, firm, ripe Anjou or Bosc pears, peeled and cored
      Vanilla ice cream or gelato

In a saucepan large enough to hold all the pears, combine the sugar with 1½ cups water. Bring to a boil and stir to dissolve the sugar. Add the wine, cinnamon sticks, honey, and ginger. Scrape in the seeds from the vanilla bean and add the bean to the saucepan. Bring the mixture to a simmer, stirring occasionally, until the honey has melted.

Add the pears and simmer over medium-low heat for 15 to 20 minutes, turning occasionally, until the pears are tender when pierced with a small knife. Remove the pears from the liquid and allow to cool. Continue to simmer the liquid until it thickens and is reduced by half, 15 to 20 minutes. Cool to room temperature. Discard the cinnamon sticks and vanilla bean.

Place each pear on a small serving plate with a scoop of vanilla ice cream. Drizzle with the poaching syrup. Serve immediately.

ricotta with vanilla-sugar croutons and berry syrup

4 SERVINGS

When I was little my grandfather used to spread fresh ricotta on a slice of bread for me and top it with a thick layer of sugar. I loved it then and I still love these flavors together. This is a somewhat healthier version of that childhood treat. The bread now plays a starring rather than supporting role in the form of sweet, crunchy croutons paired with ripe berries and creamy cheese—sooo good. Serve it for breakfast if you are feeling decadent.

croutons

- ¼ ciabatta loaf (4 ounces), cut into 1-inch cubes (4 cups)
- 3 tablespoons unsalted butter, melted
- 1½ tablespoons Vanilla Sugar (recipe follows)

berry syrup

- ½ cup fresh orange juice (from 1 medium orange)
- ¼ cup fresh lemon juice (from 1 to 2 lemons)
- ½ cup sugar
- 1 cup blueberries
- 8 strawberries, hulled and quartered

ricotta

- 1½ cups whole-milk ricotta cheese
- 3 teaspoons grated orange zest (from 1 medium orange)
- 1 teaspoon grated lemon zest (from 1 lemon)
- 1 tablespoon Vanilla Sugar (recipe follows)

Fresh mint sprigs or leaves, for garnish

For the croutons: Preheat the oven to 400°F.

In a medium bowl, toss together the bread cubes and melted butter. Add the vanilla sugar and toss to coat. Arrange the bread cubes in a single layer on

recipe continues

a parchment paper–lined rimmed baking sheet and bake until golden brown, 8 to 10 minutes. Cool completely.

For the berry syrup: In a small stainless-steel saucepan, bring the orange juice, lemon juice, and sugar to a simmer over medium-low heat. Stir until the sugar has dissolved, 2 to 3 minutes. Add the blueberries and strawberries and simmer until the fruit softens, 6 to 8 minutes. Cool the syrup to room temperature.

For the ricotta: Combine the ricotta, orange zest, lemon zest, and vanilla sugar in a medium bowl. Mix well.

To serve, divide the ricotta mixture among 4 decorative dessert bowls. Spoon the berry syrup over the ricotta and top with the croutons. Garnish with the mint sprigs or leaves.

vanilla sugar

MAKES 2 CUPS

2	cups sugar
1	vanilla bean

Pour the sugar into the bowl of a food processor. Using a paring knife, slice the vanilla bean in half, lengthwise, and scrape out the seeds. Add the vanilla seeds to the sugar. Pulse 10 to 15 times, until the vanilla and sugar are combined. Put the empty vanilla pod into a glass Mason jar. Add the vanilla sugar to the jar and seal. The sugar will keep for at least 3 months. Shake the jar before using.

espresso chip meringues
MAKES 12 MERINGUES

I dare you to stop after just one of these light and airy little treats; they melt on your tongue, leaving just a kiss of mocha flavor behind. Wait for a cool, dry day to attempt these, as humidity ruins the texture of meringues, making them grainy and gummy.

3	large egg whites, at room temperature
	Pinch of fine sea salt
3/4	cup superfine sugar (see Cook's Note)
1/8	teaspoon cream of tartar
1/4	teaspoon pure vanilla extract
2	teaspoons instant espresso powder
2/3	cup mini semisweet chocolate chips

Place an oven rack in the center of the oven and preheat the oven to 300°F. Line a baking sheet with parchment paper. Set aside.

In a stand mixer fitted with the whisk attachment, beat the egg whites and salt on medium-low speed until frothy, about 1 minute. With the machine on medium-high speed, gradually add the sugar, about 1 tablespoon at a time. Add the cream of tartar, vanilla extract, and espresso powder. Increase the speed to high and beat until the mixture is thick and holds stiff peaks, 3 to 5 minutes. Using a spatula, fold in the chocolate chips.

Drop 1/4 to 1/2 cupfuls of the mixture onto the prepared baking sheet, spacing them about 2 inches apart. Bake for 30 minutes. Rotate the pan and bake for another 30 minutes. Turn off the oven and allow the meringues to cool while still in the oven, about 2 hours.

Remove from the oven and let cool completely. Store in an airtight container for up to 4 days.

COOK'S NOTE: Superfine sugar can be found in most well-stocked supermarkets and in specialty baking stores.

apricot and nut cookies with amaretto icing

MAKES 2 TO 2½ DOZEN COOKIES

Compared to American Christmas cookies, Italian cookies are a bit less sweet. They bake up nice and buttery, and the dried apricots make them moist and chewy rather than crisp and crunchy. The dough freezes well, so I like to make a double batch and store some to bake when unexpected guests drop by (just be sure to increase the baking time by two minutes if baking from frozen). The cookies will fill the whole house with an alluring fragrance and make you look like a superstar, even if you don't have time to make the glaze.

½	cup (1 stick) unsalted butter, at room temperature
½	cup plus 2 tablespoons granulated sugar
1	teaspoon pure vanilla extract
¼	teaspoon ground cinnamon
¼	teaspoon fine sea salt
1	large egg
1¼	cups all-purpose flour
½	cup dried apricots, coarsely chopped
¼	cup slivered almonds, toasted
2	tablespoons pine nuts, toasted
1¾	cups confectioners' sugar
5	to 7 tablespoons Amaretto or other almond-flavored liqueur

In a large bowl, beat the butter, granulated sugar, vanilla extract, cinnamon, and salt with an electric mixer until light and fluffy, about 2 minutes. Beat in the egg. Stir in the flour until just blended. Mix in the apricots, almonds, and pine nuts.

Transfer the dough to a sheet of plastic wrap and shape into a log, about 12 inches long and 1½ inches in diameter. Wrap the dough in the plastic and refrigerate for 2 hours.

Preheat the oven to 350°F. Line 2 heavy baking sheets with parchment paper.

Cut the dough log crosswise into ¼- to ½-inch-thick slices. Transfer the cookies to the prepared baking sheets, spacing them 2 inches apart. Bake until the cookies are golden around the edges, about 15 minutes. Transfer the cookies to a wire rack to cool completely before icing.

To ice the cookies, pour the confectioners' sugar in a medium mixing bowl. Gradually whisk in the Amaretto until the mixture is just thin enough to drizzle.

Place the wire rack with the cookies on it over a baking sheet. Using a spoon or fork, drizzle the cookies with the icing, allowing any excess icing to drip onto the baking sheet. Allow the icing to set before serving, at least 30 minutes.

espresso caramel bars

6 TO 8 SERVINGS

Most of my desserts are fairly low-maintenance to assemble, so I hesitated to include the recipe for these in this book. But they are so incredibly irresistible and delicious—imagine a homemade candy bar with a chewy caramel center—that I decided it would be unfair not to. Take care not to overcook the caramel, so it stays soft and chewy and doesn't become hard and brittle. Investing in a candy thermometer takes away the guesswork and ensures a perfect outcome.

crust

Vegetable oil cooking spray

9   whole cinnamon graham crackers, such as Honey Maid, crumbled (1½ cups)

¼   cup light brown sugar

¾   cup (1½ sticks) unsalted butter, melted

caramel

½   cup heavy cream

½   cup (1 stick) unsalted butter, at room temperature

1½   cups light brown sugar

chocolate layer

2   cups (12 ounces) semisweet chocolate chips

½   cup heavy cream

1¾   teaspoons instant espresso powder

1   teaspoon sea salt, preferably smoked (optional)

special equipment

A candy thermometer

For the crust: Place an oven rack in the center of the oven and preheat the oven to 350°F. Spray a 7 x 10¾-inch nonstick baking pan with cooking spray. Lay a 6 x 18-inch piece of parchment paper in the pan, allowing the excess

recipe continues

paper to overhang the long sides. Spray the parchment paper lightly with cooking spray.

In the bowl of a food processor, combine the graham crackers and brown sugar. Process until the mixture resembles fine bread crumbs. Add the melted butter and blend until the mixture is combined. Spread the mixture into the bottom of the prepared pan, pressing gently to form an even layer. Bake for 10 to 12 minutes, until the edges of the crust are golden. Cool at room temperature for 10 minutes.

For the caramel: In a medium heavy-bottomed saucepan, combine the heavy cream, butter, brown sugar, and 1 tablespoon water. Stir over medium heat until the mixture is smooth. Bring the mixture to a boil and cook, without stirring, until a candy thermometer registers 240°F, 5 to 7 minutes. Carefully pour the caramel over the cooled crust. Allow the caramel layer to cool and set at room temperature, about 30 minutes.

For the chocolate layer: Combine the chocolate chips and heavy cream in a heat-proof bowl and place over a pan of gently simmering water, making sure the bottom of the pan does not touch the water. Stir until the chocolate has melted and the mixture is smooth, about 3 minutes. Whisk in the espresso powder. Pour the chocolate mixture over the caramel layer and smooth the edges with a spatula. Sprinkle the top with the sea salt, if using. Allow the chocolate layer to harden at room temperature, 1 to 2 hours.

Using a warm, damp knife, carefully cut around the edges of the dessert to free it from the pan. Using the paper overhang as handles, carefully remove it from the pan. Cut into 1-inch bars and store refrigerated in an airtight container. Allow the refrigerated bars to come to room temperature for at least 1 to 2 hours before serving.

cranberry cornmeal cake

6 TO 8 SERVINGS

Cornmeal, or polenta, is a staple ingredient in the Italian pantry and is used for both savory and sweet dishes. This not-too-sweet cake combines cranberries and orange, which remind me of the holidays—which is when I most often make this. It's one of those versatile cakes you can serve for breakfast, with tea in the afternoon, or at the end of a big meal topped with a scoop of vanilla ice cream. I like to make a few extra to give as hostess gifts.

3/4 cup (1 1/2 sticks) unsalted butter, at room temperature, plus more for the pan

1 cup all-purpose flour, plus more for the pan

1/2 cup fine yellow cornmeal

1 teaspoon baking powder

1/8 teaspoon fine sea salt

1/4 cup grated orange zest (from 2 large oranges)

3/4 cup dried cranberries, chopped into 1/4-inch pieces

1 1/4 cups sugar

1/2 teaspoon pure vanilla extract

4 large egg yolks, at room temperature

2 large eggs, at room temperature

Place an oven rack in the center of the oven and preheat the oven to 350°F. Butter and flour a 9-inch round cake pan.

In a medium bowl, whisk together the flour, cornmeal, baking powder, salt, and orange zest. Place 3 tablespoons of the flour mixture in a small bowl. Add the chopped cranberries and toss to coat.

Using a stand mixer fitted with a paddle attachment, beat the butter and sugar on medium speed until light and fluffy, about 2 minutes. Beat in the vanilla extract. Add the egg yolks and whole eggs, one at a time. Gradually add the flour mixture and mix until just incorporated. Using a spatula, gently fold in the cranberries.

Pour the batter into the prepared pan; smooth the surface with a spatula. Bake until the cake is golden and a cake tester inserted into the center comes out clean, 40 minutes. Cool for 20 minutes. Remove the cake from the pan and transfer to a wire rack to cool completely. Cut the cake into wedges and serve. (The cake can be made 1 day ahead. Store in an airtight container.)

white chocolate–dipped almond and lemon biscotti

MAKES 20 BISCOTTI

Biscotti are probably the best-known Italian sweet, and every region has its own specialty, from very simple ones flavored with anise seed to those made with flavored doughs or packed with fruits and nuts. I grew up eating biscotti made with hazelnuts and sometimes dipped in chocolate, and much as I love those, this combination of almond and lemon has become my new fave. They are crunchy and subtly flavored. For a dinner party I dip them in melted white chocolate to make them a little more special.

2	cups all-purpose flour
3/4	cup fine yellow cornmeal
1 1/2	teaspoons baking powder
1	teaspoon fine sea salt
1	cup sugar
3	large eggs
3	tablespoons grated lemon zest (from 3 to 4 lemons)
3/4	cup coarsely chopped whole almonds
2 1/2	cups (18 ounces) white chocolate chips

Preheat the oven to 325°F. Line a large baking sheet with parchment paper.

In a large bowl, whisk together the flour, cornmeal, baking powder, and salt.

In another large bowl, beat the sugar and eggs with an electric mixer until pale yellow, about 3 minutes. Mix in the lemon zest and then the flour mixture, and beat until just blended. (The dough will be sticky.) Stir in the almonds. Let the dough rest for 5 minutes.

Divide the dough evenly into 2 equal mounds and place on the prepared baking sheet. With moist hands, space the dough evenly apart and form into 2 loaves, each 9 x 3 inches. Bake for 35 minutes, or until lightly browned. Cool for 5 minutes.

Using a serrated knife, cut the logs crosswise into 3/4-inch-thick diagonal slices. Arrange the biscotti cut side up on the same baking sheet. Bake until the cookies are pale golden, about 25 minutes. Let cool completely.

Pour the chocolate chips into a heat-proof bowl. Place the bowl over a pan of gently simmering water, making sure the bottom of the pan does not touch the water. Stir until the chocolate is melted and smooth, about 3 minutes.

Dip the end of each biscotti in the chocolate. Transfer the dipped biscotti to a wire rack, set over a baking sheet, until the chocolate has hardened. Store in an airtight container.

raspberry pound cake
with vin santo cream

4 TO 6 SERVINGS

Pound cakes may not be the flashiest cakes in the baker's arsenal, but when you are craving something rich and satisfying, few things can beat them. Raspberries make this one special, with a tart tang and lovely flecks of fuchsia when you slice into the loaf. I dreamed this up for my husband, who is particularly fond of raspberries in his desserts, but now it's become a year-round favorite with us both. Try the vin santo cream on poached fruit or even in a cup of strong coffee. It's unusual but delicious.

pound cake

3/4	cup (1½ sticks) unsalted butter, at room temperature, plus more for the pan
1½	cups all-purpose flour, plus more for the pan
1	teaspoon baking powder
2	teaspoons grated orange zest (from 1 medium orange)
½	teaspoon ground cinnamon
½	teaspoon fine sea salt
1½	cups fresh raspberries, lightly mashed
1⅓	cups granulated sugar
4	large eggs, at room temperature
1	teaspoon pure vanilla extract

vin santo cream

1	cup heavy cream
½	teaspoon pure vanilla extract
3	tablespoons confectioners' sugar
3	tablespoons vin santo or Moscato wine

Place an oven rack in the lower third of the oven and preheat the oven to 350°F. Butter and flour a 9 x 5 x 3-inch nonstick loaf pan.

In a medium bowl, combine the flour, baking powder, orange zest, cinnamon, and salt. Whisk to combine. Place 3 tablespoons of the flour mixture in a small

recipe continues

bowl. Add the mashed raspberries and gently toss until coated (the mixture may clump).

In a stand mixer fitted with the paddle attachment, beat together the granulated sugar and butter until light and fluffy, about 2 minutes. With the machine running, add the eggs one at a time. Add the vanilla extract. Add the dry ingredients, a small amount at a time, mixing until just incorporated. Gently fold in the raspberries with a rubber spatula (see Cook's Note).

Pour the mixture into the prepared pan and bake until a cake tester inserted into the center of the cake comes out clean, about 1 hour. Cool for 20 minutes. Remove the cake from the pan and transfer to a wire rack to cool completely.

To make the vin santo cream: In the bowl of an electric mixer fitted with the whisk attachment, whip the heavy cream until it holds soft peaks. Add the vanilla extract, confectioners' sugar, and vin santo. Continue to whip until the cream holds stiff peaks.

Transfer the pound cake to a serving platter. Slice and serve with a dollop of the vin santo cream.

COOK'S NOTE: Make sure you barely fold in the mashed raspberries so you get a pretty marbled effect; if you mix too vigorously, the raspberries will break down and turn the pound cake purple.

chocolate rice pudding

6 TO 8 SERVINGS

Arborio rice is essentially risotto rice. I use these short grains to make classic risottos but also for this most decadent dessert. It's rich, creamy, and, most important, absolutely loaded with chocolate! When I serve this I make a very light meal so everyone has room to indulge and the pudding is the star of the show. It's a good choice if you need to make dessert ahead of time, as it keeps well in the refrigerator for several days.

5	cups whole milk
²/₃	cup Arborio rice
³/₄	cup sugar
1½	teaspoons grated orange zest (from 1 medium orange)
1	vanilla bean, split lengthwise
1	tablespoon unsweetened cocoa powder
1½	tablespoons orange liqueur
1	cup semisweet chocolate chips

In a medium heavy-bottomed saucepan, combine the milk, rice, sugar, and orange zest. Scrape in the seeds from the vanilla bean and add the bean to the saucepan. Bring the milk to a boil, stirring occasionally. Reduce the heat to medium-low and simmer, stirring frequently, until the rice is tender and the mixture thickens, 35 to 40 minutes.

Remove the pan from the heat and discard the vanilla bean. Stir the cocoa powder and orange liqueur into the mixture. Add the chocolate chips and stir until melted. Allow the mixture to cool for 10 minutes, stirring occasionally.

Spoon the rice pudding into serving bowls. Cover and refrigerate for at least 2½ to 3 hours or up to 1 day before serving.

lemon hazelnut tiramisù

Only the mascarpone and the ladyfingers in this lemony dessert give a nod to a traditional tiramisù, but my California spin on this beloved dessert is just as addictive. I think lemon makes everything taste a bit lighter (so I can eat more without feeling weighed down!), and the hazelnuts add a delicate flavor and lots of crunch. So while no one will mistake this for the original, I promise it will make anyone you serve it to very, very happy.

lemon-hazelnut syrup

½	cup fresh lemon juice (from 2 to 3 lemons)
⅔	cup sugar
½	cup hazelnut liqueur, such as Frangelico

tiramisù

½	cup toasted and skinned hazelnuts
	Grated zest of 1 lemon
2	cups heavy cream
½	teaspoon ground cinnamon
5	tablespoons sugar
1	pound mascarpone cheese, at room temperature
48	crisp Italian ladyfingers or Savoiardi cookies

For the lemon-hazelnut syrup: In a small saucepan, combine the lemon juice, ½ cup water, and the sugar over medium heat. Bring to a boil, reduce the heat, and simmer for 5 minutes, stirring occasionally, until the sugar has dissolved. Take the pan off the heat and allow the syrup to cool, about 20 minutes. Stir in the hazelnut liqueur.

For the tiramisù: In a food processor or blender, pulse the hazelnuts until finely chopped (but not a paste). Add the lemon zest and pulse once to combine. Set aside.

In the bowl of an electric mixer fitted with the whisk attachment, whip the heavy cream in a large bowl until thick. Add the cinnamon and 2 tablespoons of the sugar and continue to whip until the cream holds soft peaks. In another

recipe continues

bowl, beat together the remaining 3 tablespoons sugar and the mascarpone cheese for 30 seconds. Mix one quarter of the whipped cream into the mascarpone mixture. Using a rubber spatula, fold in the remaining whipped cream. Set aside.

Pour the lemon-hazelnut syrup into a small, shallow bowl. Dip 16 of the ladyfinger cookies in the syrup. Line the bottom of a 13 x 9 x 2-inch serving dish or other decorative serving dish with the dipped cookies, trimming the cookies, as necessary, to form an even layer. Spread one third of the mascarpone mixture over the cookies. Sprinkle with one third of the hazelnut mixture. Form 2 more identical layers, each consisting of 16 dipped ladyfinger cookies and ending with a layer of the mascarpone mixture sprinkled with the hazelnut mixture.

Cover and refrigerate for at least 6 hours or preferably overnight. Remove the tiramisù from the refrigerator at least 1 hour before serving.

limoncello granita

4 SERVINGS

Mascarpone cheese gives this dessert a smooth, creamy texture, making it more like a sherbet than an ordinary granita. Best of all, you don't need to scrape it as it freezes to create icy granules, so it's truly a snap to make. Serve it with tiny glasses of limoncello for a perfect summer dessert.

Lemon Simple Syrup (recipe follows)
1 cup (8 ounces) mascarpone cheese, at room temperature
½ cup limoncello liqueur
Pinch of fine sea salt

Combine the lemon simple syrup, mascarpone cheese, limoncello, and salt in a food processor. Process until the mixture is smooth. Pour the mixture into an 8 x 8-inch glass baking dish. Freeze for at least 4 hours or until the mixture is firm.

Using the tines of a fork, scrape the mixture into small serving bowls or glasses. Serve immediately.

lemon simple syrup

MAKES ABOUT 1½ CUPS

1 cup sugar
Grated zest and juice of 1 lemon

In a small saucepan, combine the sugar, 1 cup water, and the lemon zest and juice over medium heat. Bring to a boil, reduce the heat, and simmer for 5 minutes, stirring occasionally, until the sugar has dissolved. Remove the pan from the heat and allow the syrup to cool, about 20 minutes.

chocolate honey almond tart

6 TO 8 SERVINGS

I love desserts that transform just a few simple ingredients into a show-stopping confection. Honey gives this rich tart an intriguing, elusive flavor and floral aroma. Serve the tart in small wedges, as it is extremely rich, or cut it into little triangles to pack along on a picnic.

9	chocolate graham crackers
2	tablespoons slivered almonds
4	tablespoons (1/2 stick) unsalted butter, cut into 1/2-inch pieces, at room temperature, plus more for the pan
3/4	cup heavy cream
1/4	cup honey
2	cups (12 ounces) semisweet chocolate chips

Preheat the oven to 350°F. Butter the bottom and sides of a 9-inch round springform pan.

Place the graham crackers and almonds in the bowl of a food processor. Process until the mixture forms fine crumbs, 15 to 20 seconds. Add the butter and pulse until incorporated. Press the crumb mixture into the bottom of the prepared pan. Bake for 12 minutes. Cool to room temperature, about 20 minutes.

In a small saucepan, whisk together the heavy cream and honey over low heat until the honey has dissolved. Increase the heat to medium and bring the mixture to just below a boil. Put the chocolate chips in a medium bowl. Pour the hot cream mixture over the chocolate and stir until smooth. Pour the chocolate filling over the prepared crust. Refrigerate for at least 5 hours or preferably overnight.

Loosen the tart from the sides of the pan by running a thin metal spatula around the edge. Unmold the tart and transfer to a serving plate. Cut into wedges and serve.

pomegranate
and mint sorbet

MAKES 1 QUART

Like raspberries and chocolate, pomegranate and chocolate make a very sexy couple, and they give this sorbet a little more body and interest than your basic fruit flavors. Its sweet-tart flavor is refreshing on a hot day, and the mint syrup has a real cooling effect.

	Mint Simple Syrup (recipe follows)
2	cups 100% pomegranate juice
1	cup orange juice
1/2	cup mini semisweet chocolate chips
	Fresh mint sprigs, for garnish

special equipment

An ice cream maker

In a glass pitcher, combine the mint simple syrup, pomegranate juice, and orange juice. Pour the pomegranate mixture into an ice cream maker and freeze according to the manufacturer's instructions. During the last 10 minutes of freezing time, add the mini chocolate chips.

Scoop the sorbet into dessert bowls and garnish with fresh mint sprigs.

mint simple syrup

MAKES 1 CUP

1	cup sugar
1	packed cup fresh mint leaves

In a small saucepan, combine the sugar, 1/2 cup water, and mint leaves over medium heat. Bring to a boil, reduce the heat, and simmer, stirring occasionally, until the sugar has dissolved, 5 minutes. Remove the pan from the heat and allow the syrup to cool for 20 minutes. Strain before using.

brunch

Limoncello and Blueberry Cooler ✹

Ginger-Tea Lemonade with Basil

Sweet Basil Smoothie

Caffè Latte with Vanilla Whipped Cream ✹

Citrus Salad ✹

Mozzarella, Raspberry, and Brown Sugar Panini

Strawberry and Rosemary Scones

Crispy Parmesan Biscuits

Shaved Melon Salad with Mint Sugar

Bacon and Pancetta Potatoes ✹

Baked Provolone and Sausage Frittata

Egg-White Frittata with Lox and Arugula

Egg, Gorgonzola, and Pancetta Sandwiches ✹

Campanelle Pasta Salad ✹

Pancetta and Cinnamon Waffles

Coffee-Glazed Italian Doughnuts (Zeppole) ✹

Blueberry and Mascarpone Turnovers

Of all the contributions America has made to the culinary world that hold a special place in my heart—chocolate chip cookies and apple pie are two that come to mind—brunch might be the one I look forward to most. Pancakes and waffles, bagels and lox, omelets and eggs Benedict—I love them all, especially when they are part of a low-key get-together with a few close friends. But though you won't hear the word *brunch* spoken in Italy, the concept behind it is hardly new to Italians.

In Italy weekends are all about the leisurely lunch, a meal that can start any time after one-thirty in the afternoon and might well stretch on into the early evening. It's not the prelude to the day's activities; it's the main event, and the menu reflects that. While it may not be as elaborate as dinner, this meal is definitely more substantial than an everyday lunch and features foods you can linger over or come back to after a bit of a breather. The meal always includes a refreshing drink, like Limoncello and Blueberry Cooler (page 204), to sip over the course of the meal. It might contain a touch of alcohol (after all, it's the weekend), but it's not too potent, so you can keep on sipping even after you've pushed back from the table. Many favorite lunch dishes, such as frittatas, pasta, and zeppole, would work equally well as part of a brunch menu, and you'll find many of these to choose from in this chapter.

If Italian weekend lunches are like a dialed-back dinner, American brunch tends to be more like an amped-up breakfast, with plenty of eggs and bacon or sausage, plus something baked or starchy, some veggies, and even something sweet to top it off. I've certainly adopted aspects of the traditional American brunch, offering comfort as well as light and healthy options, each with a twist to surprise. The egg-white frittata, with lox and arugula added for both color and flavor, is like bagel and lox with ten times the protein and none of the carbs—perfect for a California crowd. Then there are scones: my heart-shaped strawberry and rosemary treats make everyone at the table feel extra-special. And I always try to include fruit in some form, whether in a simple salad, a sweet strata, or a refreshing dessert. Finally, just as they do in Italy, I offer a light, bright drink to keep topping off as the action moves from the table to the yard or into the living room to catch up on the TiVo viewing.

limoncello and blueberry cooler

4 TO 6 SERVINGS

Limoncello is a tart and refreshing lemon liqueur reminiscent of hot summer days on the island of Capri. The bright yellow and deep blue colors make this cooler lovely to serve at a summer party; make it by the pitcherful and serve over ice in tall, skinny glasses so you can see the buoyant blueberries float.

1	(750 ml) bottle limoncello liqueur, chilled
1	cup sparkling water, chilled
1	cup fresh or frozen blueberries (see Cook's Note)
5	fresh mint sprigs, lightly crushed, plus more for garnish
	Crushed ice

In a pitcher, combine the limoncello, sparkling water, blueberries, and mint sprigs. Fill highball glasses halfway with crushed ice. Pour about ½ cup of the limoncello mixture over the ice in each glass. Garnish with mint sprigs and serve.

COOK'S NOTE: If using frozen blueberries, add them to the pitcher just before serving or they can discolor the liquid.

ginger-tea lemonade
with basil

Iced tea mixed with lemonade—also called an Arnold Palmer—is incredibly refreshing. This version is made with a hit of spicy ginger syrup and basil so it tastes a bit more complex, but it's still really simple to make. You'll want to drink this all summer long.

3	black tea bags, such as English breakfast tea
2	packed cups fresh basil leaves
1⅓	cups Ginger Simple Syrup (recipe follows)
⅔	cup fresh lemon juice (from 3 to 4 lemons)
1	cup sparkling water, chilled
2	cups ice
	Lemon slices, for garnish (optional)

In a small saucepan, bring 2 cups water to a boil over high heat. Remove the pan from the heat and add the tea bags. Stir and allow the mixture to cool to room temperature, about 20 minutes. Remove the tea bags and discard.

Lay the basil leaves on a cutting board and cover with a sheet of plastic wrap. Using a rolling pin, roll over the basil to bruise the leaves. Remove the plastic wrap and add the bruised basil to the tea. Pour in the ginger simple syrup and lemon juice. Refrigerate the mixture for 1 hour.

Just before serving, add the sparkling water to the tea mixture. Place the ice in a large pitcher and pour the lemonade over the ice. Garnish with lemon slices, if using, and serve.

ginger simple syrup

MAKES 1½ CUPS

1   cup sugar
1   (3-inch) piece of fresh ginger, peeled and chopped

In a small saucepan, combine the sugar, 1 cup water, and the ginger over medium heat. Bring to a boil, reduce the heat, and simmer for 5 minutes, stirring occasionally, until the sugar has dissolved. Remove the pan from the heat and allow the syrup to cool, about 20 minutes. Strain before using.

sweet basil smoothie

4 (6-OUNCE) SERVINGS

Who knew a smoothie could be so sophisticated? Basil and lemon syrup make this one much more refined than the usual banana-berry blend, and it's delicious with savory dishes like eggs. Served on its own it's a great way to start your day on the light side.

1¼ cups plain yogurt
1   packed cup fresh basil leaves
     Lemon Zest Syrup (recipe follows)
1   cup ice

In a blender, combine the yogurt, basil, lemon zest syrup, and ice. Blend until smooth and frothy. Pour into frosted glasses and serve immediately.

lemon zest syrup

MAKES 1½ CUPS

1   cup sugar
1½   teaspoons lemon zest

In a small saucepan, combine the sugar, 1 cup water, and the lemon zest over medium heat. Bring to a boil, reduce the heat, and simmer for 5 minutes, stirring occasionally, until the sugar has dissolved. Remove the pan from the heat and allow the syrup to cool, about 20 minutes. Strain before using.

caffè latte with vanilla whipped cream

4 (8-OUNCE) SERVINGS

Caffè latte is classic Italian, and for a Sunday brunch it would be the obvious choice over a regular pot of coffee. And while vanilla whipped cream is a small departure from the way you would find it served in any Italian café, it's a nice way to make the jolt of caffeine a little richer and more special.

1¼ cups whole milk

1 cup heavy cream

1¼ cups brewed espresso

1 cup Amaretto or other almond-flavored liqueur

2 tablespoons confectioners' sugar

1 teaspoon pure vanilla extract

Combine the milk, ½ cup of the heavy cream, the espresso, and Amaretto in a medium saucepan. Place over low heat and stir constantly until hot but not boiling, 3 to 5 minutes.

In the bowl of an electric mixer fitted with the whisk attachment, whip the remaining ½ cup heavy cream until thick. Add the confectioners' sugar and vanilla. Continue to beat until the cream holds soft peaks.

To serve, pour the espresso mixture into four 8-ounce mugs. Add a dollop of vanilla whipped cream on top and serve immediately.

citrus salad

4 TO 6 SERVINGS

Brunch is a funny meal; many of the main dishes are sweet enough to make dessert seem almost redundant. That's why I like to serve this dish, which is bright and fresh from the citrus with a hint of licorice from the fennel. It bridges the gap between salad and dessert, ending the meal on a sweet but not heavy note.

2	large oranges
2	grapefruits
1	large or 2 small fennel bulbs, trimmed and thinly sliced
½	cup olive oil
¼	cup packed fresh basil leaves
	Salt and freshly ground black pepper
⅓	cup chopped walnuts, toasted

Peel and trim the ends from the oranges and grapefruits with a sharp knife. Place a sieve over a medium bowl. Hold an orange over the bowl and, using a paring knife, cut along the membrane on both sides of each segment. Free the segments and let them fall into the sieve. Repeat with the remaining orange and the grapefruits. Squeeze the membranes over the bowl to extract as much juice as possible, reserving the juices in the bottom of the bowl. Place the citrus segments and fennel in a salad bowl.

In a blender or the bowl of a small food processor, blend together the oil, basil, and 3 tablespoons of the reserved juice until smooth. Season with salt and pepper. Pour over the fruit and fennel. Add the chopped walnuts and toss until all the ingredients are coated.

mozzarella, raspberry, and brown sugar panini

4 SERVINGS

This brunch dish brings together sweet and savory flavors in a way that is insanely good. The cheese melts into the raspberry jam and, combined with the brown sugar, makes this surprisingly addictive.

8	(½-inch-thick) slices bakery-style white bread
¼	cup olive oil
½	cup raspberry jam
2	teaspoons chopped fresh rosemary leaves
8	ounces fresh mozzarella cheese, drained and patted dry
	Salt (optional)
2	tablespoons light brown sugar

special equipment

A panini press, indoor grill, or ridged grill pan (see Cook's Note)

Preheat the panini press or indoor grill.

Using a pastry brush, brush the bread on both sides with the oil. Spread one side of each slice of bread with the raspberry jam. Sprinkle the rosemary over the jam. Cut the mozzarella cheese into 8 slices. Place 2 slices of cheese on each of 4 of the bread slices. Season the cheese with a pinch of salt, if using. Place the remaining slices of bread on top, jam side down. Sprinkle the tops with the brown sugar.

Grill the panini for 3 to 5 minutes, until the cheese has melted and the bread is golden and crispy. Cut the panini in half and serve.

COOK'S NOTE: If you do not have a panini press or indoor grill, use a ridged grill pan: Preheat the pan, add the sandwiches (in batches, if necessary), and put a weight (such as a brick wrapped in aluminum foil or a heavy cast-iron skillet) on top to press them down. Grill for 2 to 3 minutes to brown the first side, flip the sandwich, replace the weight, and grill for 2 to 3 minutes to brown the other side and finish melting the cheese.

strawberry and rosemary scones

MAKES 14 SCONES

The combination of strawberry jam and piney rosemary may sound strange, but together they add up to the perfect blend of sweet and savory—and these scones, which are a bit lighter in texture than regular ones, smell incredible as they bake. I think using a heart-shaped biscuit cutter makes them even prettier.

2	cups all-purpose flour, plus more for dusting
½	cup granulated sugar
2	teaspoons baking powder
1	tablespoon finely chopped fresh rosemary leaves
¼	teaspoon fine sea salt
6	tablespoons (¾ stick) cold unsalted butter, cut into ½-inch pieces
1	cup heavy cream
⅓	cup strawberry jam
¼	cup fresh lemon juice (from 1 to 2 lemons)
2	cups confectioners' sugar

Place an oven rack in the middle of the oven and preheat the oven to 375°F. Line a baking sheet with parchment paper. Set aside.

In the bowl of a food processor, pulse together the flour, granulated sugar, baking powder, rosemary, salt, and butter until the mixture resembles a coarse meal. With the machine running, gradually pour in the heavy cream and process until the mixture forms a dough.

On a lightly floured work surface, roll out the dough into a 10-inch circle that's ½ inch thick. Using a 3-inch heart-shaped or similarly sized cookie cutter, cut out pieces of dough and place on the prepared baking sheet. Gently knead together any leftover pieces of dough and roll out to ½ inch thick. Cut the dough with the cutter and place on the baking sheet. Using your index finger or a small, round measuring spoon, gently make an indentation in the center of each scone. Spoon a heaped ½ teaspoon of jam into each indentation.

Bake for 18 to 20 minutes, or until the edges of the scones are golden brown. Transfer the cooked scones onto a wire rack. Cool for 30 minutes.

In a medium bowl, mix together the lemon juice and confectioners' sugar until smooth. Gradually add 1 to 2 tablespoons water until the mixture is thin enough to drizzle. Using a spoon, drizzle the glaze over the scones. Place the scones on a wire rack for about 30 minutes until the glaze has set. Store in an airtight container for up to 2 days.

COOK'S NOTE: The dough can also be made by hand by stirring together the flour, sugar, baking powder, rosemary, and salt in a large mixing bowl. Add the butter. Using your fingertips or a pastry blender, work the butter into the flour until the mixture resembles a coarse meal. Gradually stir in the heavy cream until the mixture forms a dough.

crispy parmesan biscuits

MAKES 12 BISCUITS

I've given an American Southern staple an Italian spin with the addition of Parmesan. The cornmeal makes these biscuits sturdy enough to pack on a picnic, and you can stuff them with smoked salmon (my fave), sliced turkey or ham, or even grilled veggies. Hot out of the oven, they are pretty terrific with just a bit of lemon butter.

1½	cups all-purpose flour
½	cup fine yellow cornmeal
½	teaspoon fine sea salt
2	teaspoons baking powder
1	teaspoon baking soda
4	tablespoons (½ stick) cold unsalted butter, cut into ½-inch cubes
2	cups (5½ ounces) freshly grated Parmesan cheese
½	cup finely chopped scallions, white and green parts
¾	cup buttermilk
⅓	cup olive oil
½	cup Lemon Butter (recipe follows), at room temperature
3	cups (3 ounces) baby arugula
10	ounces smoked salmon or prosciutto

Place an oven rack in the center of the oven and preheat the oven to 400°F. Line a baking sheet with parchment paper.

In a medium bowl, combine the flour, cornmeal, salt, baking powder, and baking soda. Add the butter. Using your fingertips or a pastry blender, work the butter into the flour until the mixture resembles a coarse meal. Stir in the Parmesan cheese and scallions. Add the buttermilk and olive oil. Stir until the mixture forms a dough.

Drop the dough onto the prepared baking sheet in 12 equal-size pieces. Bake for 18 to 20 minutes, or until golden. Cool the biscuits for 10 minutes, then transfer to a rack to cool completely.

Slice each biscuit in half and spread each half with 1 teaspoon lemon butter. Add some arugula leaves and place a small slice of smoked salmon or prosciutto on top. Add the top half of the biscuit and serve.

lemon butter

MAKES ½ CUP

½ cup (1 stick) unsalted butter, at room temperature
   Grated zest of 1 lemon

In a small bowl, mash the butter and lemon zest together using a fork. Cover and refrigerate until ready to use. Bring to room temperature before serving.

shaved melon salad
with mint sugar

4 TO 6 SERVINGS

This salad looks like *tricolore* papardelle pasta, with vibrant ribbons of pink, green, and orange melon. If you don't want to bother to make the melon shavings, just use a melon baller or cut the fruit in cubes; the salad will still be beautiful. This is one that both children and adults go nuts for, and the mint gives it an extra burst of freshness.

- 1/2 (about 1 pound) small seedless watermelon (see Cook's Note)
- 1/2 (about 1 pound) honeydew melon (see Cook's Note), seeds removed
- 1/2 (about 1 pound) cantaloupe melon (see Cook's Note), seeds removed
- 1/2 cup packed fresh mint leaves, finely chopped, plus mint sprigs, for garnish
- 1/2 cup turbinado or other coarse sugar

Cut each melon lengthwise into 1-inch-wide slices. Hold the melon slices at the peel end and, using a sharp vegetable peeler, shave the melon flesh in long ribbons into a large serving bowl.

In a small bowl, combine the mint leaves and sugar. Add the mint sugar to the shaved melon and gently toss.

Arrange the melon salad on individual salad plates. Garnish with fresh mint sprigs and serve.

COOK'S NOTE: The melons are easiest to shave into ribbons when they are slightly underripe and chilled.

bacon and pancetta potatoes

4 SERVINGS

Adding both bacon and pancetta to these potatoes may seem like overkill, but trust me—they pack a great one-two punch. The bacon gives the potatoes a smoky flavor, and the pancetta lends meaty substance. These go quickly, so make a double recipe or you'll find yourself with an empty serving dish before you know it.

4	slices thick-cut bacon, coarsely chopped
2	(¼-inch-thick) slices pancetta, cut into ¼-inch pieces
3	medium russet potatoes, peeled and cut into ½-inch cubes
1	garlic clove, thinly sliced
	Salt and freshly ground black pepper
2	tablespoons coarsely chopped fresh thyme leaves

Heat a large nonstick skillet over medium heat. Add the bacon and pancetta. Cook, stirring occasionally, until the bacon and pancetta are brown and crispy, 10 to 12 minutes. Using a slotted spoon, remove the bacon and pancetta pieces and drain on paper towels.

Add the potatoes and garlic to the pan. Season with ¼ teaspoon salt and ¼ teaspoon pepper. Cook, stirring frequently, until the potatoes are golden and cooked through, 20 to 25 minutes.

Add the thyme, bacon, and pancetta to the skillet. Cook for 5 minutes. Season with salt and pepper.

Transfer the potatoes to a large serving bowl. Serve immediately.

baked provolone and sausage frittata

4 TO 6 SERVINGS

If you have eggs, milk, and some kind of cheese in the fridge, you have the basics for a frittata, making this a perfect spur-of-the-moment recipe. Substitute just about any leftover ingredients you have on hand for the sausage and provolone; the more you experiment, the more fun this is!

Unsalted butter, for the baking dish

2	tablespoons olive oil
1	small onion, diced
½	pound mild turkey sausage, casings removed
8	large eggs
⅓	cup whole milk
1½	teaspoons salt
1	red bell pepper, cored, seeded, and diced
3	cups (8 ounces) shredded provolone cheese
¼	cup plus 2 tablespoons chopped fresh flat-leaf parsley leaves

Place an oven rack in the center of the oven and preheat the oven to 425°F. Lightly butter an 8-inch-square glass baking dish.

Heat the oil in a medium skillet over medium-high heat. Add the onion and cook until translucent, about 3 minutes. Add the sausage and cook until brown, about 5 minutes. Set aside to cool.

In a large bowl, whisk together the eggs, milk, and salt until smooth, about 20 seconds. Add the bell pepper, 2 cups of the cheese, and ¼ cup parsley. Stir in the onion mixture. Pour the mixture into the prepared baking dish. Sprinkle with the remaining 1 cup cheese. Bake for 20 to 25 minutes, or until set and golden brown.

Slide the frittata onto a serving platter. Using a serrated knife, cut the frittata into wedges and sprinkle with the remaining 2 tablespoons parsley before serving.

COOK'S NOTE: To make individual servings, divide the batter among 4 buttered 8-ounce ramekins. Bake for 15 to 18 minutes, or until set and golden brown.

egg-white frittata
with lox and arugula

4 TO 6 SERVINGS

Frittatas are the perfect centerpiece for a brunch spread because they can be served warm or at room temperature. This one brings two classic brunch favorites—lox and eggs—together into one very attractive dish. Serving bagels on the side, though decidedly not Italian, is a nice option.

8	large egg whites, at room temperature
1/2	cup heavy cream
6	ounces lox or smoked salmon, chopped into 1/2-inch pieces
	Grated zest of 1 lemon
1/2	teaspoon salt
1/2	teaspoon freshly ground black pepper
2	tablespoons olive oil
2	packed cups (2 ounces) arugula
1	garlic clove, minced

Place an oven rack in the center of the oven and preheat the oven to 350°F.

In a medium bowl, whisk the egg whites until fluffy, about 30 seconds. Add the heavy cream, lox, lemon zest, salt, and pepper.

In a 10-inch ovenproof nonstick skillet, heat the oil over medium heat. Add the arugula and garlic. Cook, stirring frequently, until the arugula has wilted, about 1 minute. Pour the egg mixture into the pan and stir to combine the ingredients. Cook, without stirring, for 4 minutes. Place the skillet in the oven and bake for 10 to 12 minutes, until the frittata is set.

Slide the frittata onto a platter. Using a serrated knife, cut the frittata into wedges and serve warm or at room temperature.

egg, gorgonzola, and pancetta sandwiches

4 SERVINGS

I have a big pet peeve with most egg salads: too many are loaded with mayo, which ruins their texture and makes them bland. My version still has a little mayo, but I add mild Gorgonzola and lemon zest, which not only brings a classic Italian flavor and freshness to the sandwich but also keeps the salad moist. Crispy pancetta makes this recipe brunch-worthy, and while you can certainly substitute bacon, it's a lot less Italian that way.

	Vegetable oil cooking spray
12	very thin slices of pancetta
6	hard-boiled eggs, peeled and coarsely chopped
1	cup (4 ounces) crumbled Gorgonzola cheese
	Grated zest of 1 lemon
1/3	cup mayonnaise
1/3	cup chopped fresh chives
	Salt and freshly ground black pepper
8	(1/2-inch-thick) slices whole wheat bread

Place an oven rack in the center of the oven and preheat the oven to 400°F.

Spray a rimmed baking sheet with cooking spray. Lay the pancetta in a single layer on the prepared baking sheet and bake for 10 to 12 minutes, until crispy and brown. Drain on paper towels.

In a medium bowl, combine the eggs, Gorgonzola cheese, lemon zest, mayonnaise, and chives. Season with salt and pepper. Spread the mixture evenly over 4 slices of the bread. Crumble the pancetta and sprinkle over the egg mixture. Place the remaining bread slices on top.

Cut the sandwiches in half and arrange on a serving platter.

campanelle pasta salad

4 TO 6 SERVINGS

An Italian brunch wouldn't be complete without a pasta dish. Campanelle pasta is named for the church bells it resembles, and the nooks and crannies are great for trapping sauce, making every bite delicious. If you can't find campanelle, any small shaped pasta will do. There are lots of bold flavors in this pasta salad, the base of which is canned tuna. Although it's definitely more caloric, tuna packed in olive oil rather than water gives the salad a much fuller, richer flavor.

1	pound campanelle pasta
½	cup olive oil
1	small red onion, chopped
2	garlic cloves, minced
1	(6-ounce) can Italian tuna in oil, such as Flott, drained
1	pint (2 cups) cherry tomatoes, halved
8	ounces frozen artichoke hearts, thawed and quartered
2	tablespoons capers, rinsed and drained
2	tablespoons chopped fresh thyme leaves
¼	cup chopped fresh flat-leaf parsley leaves
	Salt and freshly ground black pepper

Bring a large pot of salted water to a boil over high heat. Add the pasta and cook, stirring occasionally, until tender but still firm to the bite, 8 to 10 minutes. Drain the pasta, reserving about 1 cup of the pasta water.

In a 14-inch skillet, heat ¼ cup of the oil over medium-high heat. Add the onion and cook, stirring frequently, until soft, about 5 minutes. Add the garlic and cook for 30 seconds, or until aromatic. Add the tuna to the skillet and, using a fork, break it into chunks. Add the cherry tomatoes, artichoke hearts, capers, and thyme. Cook, stirring occasionally, until the tomatoes begin to soften, 8 to 10 minutes.

Add the pasta, the remaining ¼ cup olive oil, and the parsley. Toss until all the ingredients are coated, adding a little pasta water, if needed, to thin out the sauce. Season with salt and pepper. Transfer the pasta salad to a serving bowl and serve warm or at room temperature.

pancetta and cinnamon waffles

4 TO 6 SERVINGS

I never really had waffles growing up in Italy, but Todd *loves* them, so when we got together I knew I had to find a way to incorporate them into our breakfast routine. The result is an impressive-looking brunch dish with all the elements I think a great waffle should have: these are salty, sweet, and crunchy in every bite.

$^1/_2$ cup chopped walnuts

1   tablespoon olive oil

3   (4-ounce) slices of pancetta, each about $^1/_4$ inch thick, diced into $^1/_4$-inch pieces

3   cups Belgian waffle mix, such as Krusteaz

2   large eggs

$^1/_3$ cup vegetable oil, plus more for the waffle iron

$1^1/_2$ teaspoons ground cinnamon

$^1/_2$ teaspoon salt

$^1/_2$ cup pure maple syrup, warm

special equipment

A Belgian or conventional waffle iron

Preheat the oven to 350°F.

Spread the walnuts in an even layer on a rimmed baking sheet. Bake for 10 to 12 minutes, until toasted and fragrant. Set aside to cool.

Preheat and lightly grease a waffle iron.

Heat the olive oil in a medium skillet over medium-high heat. Add the pancetta and cook until brown and crispy, 3 to 5 minutes. Transfer the pancetta to a paper towel–lined plate to cool.

In a large mixing bowl, combine the waffle mix, eggs, vegetable oil, 1½ cups water, the cinnamon, and salt. Using a whisk, blend the ingredients together until smooth. Stir in the pancetta. Pour the batter, using the amount recommended by the waffle iron manufacturer's instructions, into the preheated waffle iron. Cook waffles for 3 to 4 minutes, or until golden brown.

Place the waffles onto serving plates. Sprinkle with the chopped walnuts and drizzle with the maple syrup. Serve immediately.

coffee-glazed italian doughnuts (zeppole)

MAKES ABOUT 12 DOUGHNUTS; 4 TO 6 SERVINGS

If your only impression of a zeppole was formed at a street fair, where they are served hot out of the oil and dusted with powdered sugar, prepare to have your socks knocked off. With these you get your doughnut and coffee all in one delectable bite.

doughnuts

½	cup (1 stick) unsalted butter, cut into ½-inch pieces, at room temperature
¼	cup granulated sugar
¼	teaspoon fine sea salt
1	cup all-purpose flour
3	large eggs
1	large egg yolk
2	teaspoons grated lemon zest (from 1 to 2 lemons)
	Vegetable oil, for frying

glaze

¼	cup heavy cream
1	tablespoon coffee liqueur, such as Kahlúa
2	teaspoons instant espresso powder
2	cups confectioners' sugar
1	(3-ounce) bittersweet or semisweet chocolate bar
1	cup raspberries

For the doughnuts: In a medium saucepan, combine the butter, ½ cup water, the granulated sugar, and salt over medium heat. Bring to a rolling boil, stirring occasionally. Boil for 10 seconds. Remove the pan from the heat and add the flour. Using a wooden spoon, quickly stir the mixture until all the flour is fully incorporated and forms a thick dough. Return the pan to the heat and stir continuously for 2 minutes.

recipe continues

Scrape the mixture into a stand mixer fitted with a paddle attachment. With the machine running on medium speed, add the eggs and egg yolk, one at a time, mixing until fully incorporated. Beat the mixture for 4 to 5 minutes, until thick and glossy. Add the lemon zest and beat until smooth. Refrigerate the dough for 15 minutes.

For the glaze: In a medium bowl, whisk together the cream, coffee liqueur, and espresso powder until smooth. With a wooden spoon, gradually stir in the confectioners' sugar until smooth. If the glaze is too thick, stir in water, ¼ teaspoon at a time.

In a large, heavy-bottomed saucepan, pour enough oil to fill the pan about a third of the way. Heat over medium heat until a deep-frying thermometer inserted in the oil reaches 375°F. (If you don't have a thermometer, toss in a cube of bread; it will brown in about 3 minutes and, when it does, the oil is ready.)

Using a small ice cream scoop or two small spoons, carefully drop about 1 tablespoon of the dough at a time into the oil. Cook for 3 to 3½ minutes, turning occasionally, until the doughnuts are golden and puffed. Drain on paper towels. When the doughnuts are cool enough to handle, dip the top halves into the glaze.

Using a hand grater, grate the chocolate over serving plates. Place 3 to 4 doughnuts on each plate and garnish with raspberries. Serve immediately.

blueberry and mascarpone turnovers

MAKES 12 TURNOVERS

Golden brown on the outside, melting and sweet on the inside, these are best hot, right out of the pan, but they hold up even after they have cooled. It's fine to use frozen blueberries for the filling, but be sure to thaw and drain them first or they will turn the cheese filling an unappealing gray.

½	cup (4 ounces) mascarpone cheese, at room temperature
2	tablespoons sugar, plus more for sprinkling
½	teaspoon cornstarch
1	teaspoon grated lemon zest (from 1 lemon)
1	teaspoon fresh lemon juice
⅓	cup fresh or thawed frozen blueberries, drained
2	(9-inch) refrigerated rolled pie crusts
1	large egg, beaten
	Vegetable oil, for frying

special equipment

A 3½-inch round cookie cutter

In a small bowl, mix together the mascarpone cheese, sugar, cornstarch, lemon zest, and lemon juice until smooth. Stir in the blueberries.

Using the cookie cutter, cut the pie crusts into 12 circles. Place the dough circles on a parchment paper–lined baking sheet. Using a pastry brush, lightly brush the edges of each piece of dough with the egg. Spoon about 1½ teaspoons of the cheese mixture in the center of each circle. Fold the dough in half to enclose the filling and pinch the edges to seal. Using the tines of a fork, gently crimp the sealed edges. Refrigerate for 10 minutes.

In a large, heavy-bottomed saucepan, pour enough oil to fill the pan about a third of the way. Heat over medium heat until a deep-frying thermometer inserted in the oil reaches 375°F. (If you don't have a thermometer, toss in a cube of bread; it will brown in about 3 minutes and, when it does, the oil is ready.) Fry the turnovers, turning once, for 1 to 1½ minutes, until golden.

Drain on paper towels and sprinkle with sugar while still hot. Cool for at least 10 minutes before serving.

acknowledgments

For the time and effort that was devoted to creating this cookbook and bringing my family recipes to life, I offer my heartfelt appreciation to these amazing and talented people.

To Jonelle Weaver and her assistant, Marianne Campolongo, a special thanks for working your magic with the camera—the photos are beautiful. Valerie Aikman-Smith and her assistant, Michele Chase, for making my food look like you'd want to eat it right off the page. Robin Turk, and her assistant, April Smith, for your vision in prop styling. Julie Morgan, for making me camera-pretty, and Veronica Lane Garcia, for making my friends and family camera-pretty. Eric and Maxine Greenspan, for use of your lovely home. Karen Krasner, for the generous use of your studio.

Andy Sheen-Turner, for your patience and dedication to testing and retesting recipes. Rica Allannic, for your editorial talent and allowing this book to become a true reflection of who I am. Marysarah Quinn, for your artistic vision. And Pam Krauss, for your guidance and continued friendship.

To the special people in my life who support and protect me: Suzanne Gluck, Jon Rosen, Eric Greenspan, Christine Tripicchio, Sandra Tripicchio, and Diana Bassett. You have my absolute gratitude for all you do.

To my family: You've inspired these recipes, and I thank you and love you for your unending support.

Finally, to my husband, Todd, and my daughter, Jade. You are the reasons I love what I do and look forward to the journey ahead.

credits

Alex Marshall Studios

Fissler USA

Mel Gragirena Woodworks

Micucci

index

Note: Page references in *italics* refer to photographs.